FOUNDATIONS FOR READING: INFORMAL PRE-READING PROCEDURES

FOUNDATIONS
FOR READING

informal pre-reading procedures

Marion Monroe and Bernice Rogers

SCOTT, FORESMAN AND COMPANY   *Chicago, Atlanta, Dallas, Palo Alto, Fair Lawn, N.J.*

45888

Of all the areas of American education that have been given attention in the popular press during the last decade it would be difficult to find one that has received such generous coverage as have methods of teaching beginning reading. Almost every popular magazine has carried one or more articles on this subject, often presenting some supposedly brand new panacea for all the ills that, it is said, beset the public schools in their task of teaching reading. If only the teacher would use such-and-such a new device or technique, all problems would be solved, they imply, and all children, regardless of individual differences, would be launched on a successful road to reading.

With all this pressure from the popular press, it is no wonder that parents have become puzzled and in many cases aroused, directing their dissatisfactions toward the classroom teacher who may herself be puzzled and misled by much of the popular and often irresponsible material presented.

Only the teacher who has had a thorough, systematic grounding in the methods of building foundation reading skills is in a position to evaluate the constant barrage of materials on reading, to sift the superficial and the spurious from the responsible and constructive, and to plan and carry through her own day-to-day program with confidence and success. To give prospective teachers this kind of understanding of the business of learning to read, *Foundations for Reading* has been prepared.

Foundations for Reading covers the pre-reading period, providing guidance for the teacher from the time the beginner first comes to school until he is ready to read printed language. Used as a textbook in a reading methods course, or in a general elementary or primary methods course, it will do several important things to prepare the teacher to cope with the problems of this crucial period.

First it will help to clarify the relationship between many aspects of child growth and development and the process of learning to read. Many times the teacher of beginning reading is baffled and discouraged by the fact that her pupils, all apparently starting from the same point, i.e., non-reading, move forward at such vastly different rates. *Foundations for Reading* explains the relation of many kinds of pre-school experiences and pre-school growth to the degree and kind of readiness the child may have for learning to read. It identifies the various sensory skills, and the various thinking patterns, habits, and attitudes that function in learning to read, and explains how these various skills, habits, and attitudes form a basis for the more complex reading skills shortly to be learned.

Another kind of help provided in *Foundations for Reading* is in the area of specific activity suggestions. Understanding the tool skills needed in reading is the teacher's necessary basis for planning instruction, but theory is not enough. *Foundations for Reading* has been designed to help the teacher see the relation between theory of instruction and the specific day-to-day activities that will facilitate learning progress in her classroom. Each activity presented in the book is described in relation to an explanation of the skill it is designed to develop or strengthen, and in relation to other activities that focus on the same skill. This method of presentation of activities will, it is hoped, enable the teacher to select and plan activities for daily instruction in logical sequence and in combinations suitable to the designated learning goals, and to the child's own level of development.

The major focus of *Foundations for Reading* is on the developmental reading program for the classroom. There is also, however, in addition to the developmental material, one chapter (Chapter 7) to which the teacher may refer for help with her "problem" children. This chapter does not presume to provide all the answers in this complex area. It makes some suggestions that can be followed by the classroom teacher, suggests in some cases where answers may be found, and identifies the kinds of problems the teacher may be able to handle and those that should be referred to other professional specialists for diagnosis and treatment.

Foundations for Reading is a revision of Dr. Monroe's book, *Growing Into Reading*. Its new organization and focus will, it is hoped, make it easier for the classroom teacher to apply suggested activity and evaluation techniques in her own daily instructional program. In addition, new research and new viewpoints have been drawn upon to bring the book up to date.

The authors hope that the new *Foundations for Reading* will enable many more teachers to incorporate into their daily procedures at pre-reading level the skill-oriented and goal-directed activities that constitute the real foundations for learning to read.

Contents

chapter one

Where Reading Begins

The sun rose with a new brightness on the morning of a new day—a very special day, not at all like other days. One little boy even forgot to finish drinking his milk at breakfast. This was not too surprising, because how could anyone remember to finish milk on the day when he was going to school for the very first time!

For the child this is the beginning of a great new epoch. He's going to school like the big boys and girls. And what is more, he's going to learn to do something completely new—he's going to learn to read!

This is a very special morning for someone else too. It's a special morning for his teacher who is about to meet a roomful of entirely new first-graders who will come to her with personalities and backgrounds as variable as the clouds of the sky, but with one thing in common—they will all expect her to teach them how to read.

BRIDGING THE GAP FROM
SPEECH TO PRINT

The teacher sees the situation somewhat differently from her pupils. The boys and girls think they're going to start something entirely new. But the teacher knows that they are not starting something completely new, as they suppose, but rather that they are going to build a set of more refined and more complex language skills based on the language experiences they have had already.

Until now the children's language experiences have been almost entirely with the spoken language: hearing it, associating meaning with it, speaking it. A little boy knows, for instance, what his mother means when she says, "Timetogotobed." Sometimes he doesn't go. He knows what she means when she says, "Putthekittydown." Sometimes he doesn't do this, either. Then there are all sorts of sounds, all with their own meanings, like "Comere." And how about "Dontgoin-themud" and "Stayoutofthemud"? "Mud" has a meaning all by itself: squishy, soft, wet, nice. The rest, no matter how it sounds, means "NO."

Building on countless language experiences like these—different for each child—the teacher is going to teach her boys and girls to get meaning out of little black words printed on white paper. One little boy at least won't have trouble with the word *mud*. Now *that* is something he knows all about!

But it won't all be that simple. Language is spoken language, and the written form is only the transcription of the spoken language. But for boys and girls starting to school, there will sometimes seem to be a tremendous difference between what they have heard and what the teacher tells them the book says. Not all of them will know, for example, that "Comere" is two words. And how can "What do you see?" be the same thing as "Whaddya see?"

The teacher has to help all her children bridge this gap from speech to print. For some children it will be only a small step. For others it will be a giant-sized stride. The size and nature of the gap will depend on the kind of language experiences each child has had previous to that special day when he first comes to school.

LANGUAGE EXPERIENCES OF
THE PRESCHOOL CHILD

How has each child's language developed during the preschool years? What has been the process of language
growth from birth until formal instruction begins? There
are those who view the child's acquisition of his mother
tongue as one of the most impressive achievements of
human life. Yet because the process is so gradual and so
universal, many people are inclined to overlook it. Psychologists who have had an opportunity to observe and
record the language behavior of many children have been
able to formulate some descriptions of language behavior
for certain age levels. Under conditions in which books
were present in the child's environment, they have also been
able to observe and describe book behavior at various age
levels. Observing the behavior of many children, they have
been able to generalize what is usually done by a child
of a certain age group. Of course, no child conforms
exactly to this generalized growth pattern; each child is
an individual with his own individual way of growing.
But some generalizations are helpful in thinking about the
growth process and about the sequence of developmental
events which take place as a child learns to use language.

The following descriptions of such generalized growth
patterns will give background for understanding the language base on which the teacher of beginning reading
builds. Beyond indicating that differences exist, no attempt
is made in this section to describe the range of individual
differences found at each age level. Some of the individual
differences and their causes are discussed in Chapter 2 and
in subsequent chapters of this book.

The first year

The newborn infant enters the world with a cry that is
his first use of the physical apparatus for producing speech.
The birth cry is the rush of air over the vocal cords.
After this first reflexive vocalization, several stages of
growth take place before the infant is ready and able to
speak the first meaningful word.

The month-old infant expresses his needs and feelings by crying. He may vaguely differentiate the crying sounds associated with hunger, discomfort, or pain. A loving and attentive mother often reports that she can detect slight differences in the crying sounds that indicate whether she should take the baby his bottle, change his diaper, or burp him, although to most listeners all infant crying at this stage sounds alike.

Between six and eight weeks, the baby also cries for social stimulation, and he is quieted if picked up or brought out where he can see people and hear voices. At three or four months, he not only cries but coos, gurgles, and laughs aloud. He "talks" to his mother, answering her voice with soft little sounds. He also "talks" to himself, cooing contentedly in his crib or buggy even when no one is about for him to see or hear. Vocalization is used not only as a response to social situations but as a satisfying means of self-expression even when the baby is alone.

Various studies have been made of the order of appearance of speech sounds—vowels and consonants—in infant crying and cooing. These studies indicate that the earliest speech sounds are vowels and that consonants soon follow. The baby experiments with sounds and may make almost any possible speech sound. He may make vowel and consonant sounds that will not be needed in his mother tongue —sounds which will gradually be eliminated as he finds out that no one responds to them.

At about six months, the baby's articulation becomes more imitative of the sounds he hears in the language of his home. He combines vowels and consonants into syllables such as "da-da-da." Sometimes a chance combination of sounds may resemble a true word, but, unless the infant gives the same response in a similar situation, it is doubtful that he has associated the conventional meaning with the chance utterance.

From six to twelve months of age, the baby listens more attentively and adjusts to certain familiar words. He usually learns to do a few little tricks at about nine months, in response to verbal directions. For example, he may learn to clap his hands when he hears "pat-a-cake," he may wave his hand when his mother says "bye-bye," or he may stop crying and show eagerness when he hears "Want your bottle?" Between nine and twelve months, he shows an increasing responsiveness to language, and his parents begin to pick out the words he seems to understand and hopefully coax him: "Say pat-a-cake," "Say bye-bye," "Say bottle," "Say Daddy," and so on.

Occasionally a baby will say his first word so unexpectedly and dramatically that the occasion is well remembered and dated. More frequently, the first word emerges so gradually from the many babbling attempts, failures, and partial successes that parents are unable to recall an exact date when the baby began to talk. Most parents report that talking seems to begin when the infant says a word or two "around twelve months."

What may be referred to as "book behavior" has also been recorded, and it may be said to begin at about a year if there are any books in the child's environment. At twelve months, most infants give merely fleeting attention to books except to regard the book as one of the many fascinating objects in the environment to be mouthed, manipulated, dropped, and regained. Paper is crumpled, torn, brought to the mouth. Books are pushed through the bars of a playpen, and the problem of getting back the book occupies more attention than the book itself. Old magazines are enjoyed for the fun of tearing paper. A year-old infant spends many happy moments of the day in his playpen tearing out magazine pages, crumpling, mouthing, stamping them with his feet until he has surrounded himself with a litter of shredded paper. During such activity he may give momentary attention to a portion of a picture, attracted primarily by its brightness.

When books are present in the immediate environment, the following concepts may have developed by the age of twelve months:

Book as an object: Books are made of interesting material having certain distinctive textures (tactile sensations) and qualities (can be torn, crumpled, or otherwise manipulated).

Content of book: Books contain bright-colored patterns that are part of the paper. A few twelve-month-old infants appear to recognize pictures of simple, familiar objects, especially if the picture is photographic in detail and colored accurately.

Printed symbols: No notice is given to printing.

From twelve months to fifteen months

Between twelve and fifteen months of age, children practice "talking." They are attracted by and interested in the flowing sounds of language, with all its inflections and expressions. They imitate these sounds and also attempt to say more and more isolated words. The toddler's jargon at this age takes on the inflections of actual speech, so that a hearer in another room may receive the impression that the child is actually talking. His prattling has a sentence-like quality, and his tone of voice is now demanding, now questioning, sometimes scolding, sometimes conversational. Inserted into this flow of jargon are the few but growing number of words he can pronounce.

There are wide individual differences in the amount of jargon used by youngsters in this age group. The quiet child may use very little of it. He may wait until he is able to pronounce a word and then use it with sentence-like finality. "Up" may mean "Please take me up on your lap." The little chatterbox, on the other hand, "talks" fluently in expressive babbling, in which actual words are increasingly evident, until one day the parents realize that the jargon has practically disappeared and the child is really talking. Individual differences may result partly from innate factors and partly from environment. Some mothers talk to their babies much more than other mothers. One mother said, "I seldom talk to him (her fourteen-month-old son), because I'd feel foolish talking to a person who can't reply. Sometimes I say 'cup' when I give him a cup, or 'orange juice,' and so on, so he will know the names of things. We are usually a quiet pair when just the two of us are alone."

Another mother said, "We have the most delightful conversations. I talk to him (her twelve-month-old son) all the time, and he 'talks' right back to me. He's so much company that I never get lonesome any more. The minute he wakes up he starts jabbering, and we both keep it up most of the day."

At about fifteen months, the infant develops a growing interest in the pictures in books. If his mother has time to read to him, he will enjoy sitting on her lap, looking at colored pictures while she turns the pages. He may become absorbed in the page-turning activity and try to turn the pages himself. He still lapses frequently into the tearing and manipulative activities of the twelve-month-old infant, especially if he has not had ample opportunity for this type of exploration in the past. He becomes attached to a cloth, cardboard, or plastic book that will stand up under the battering he gives it, and he carries it around at times just as he does other favorite toys. He shows recognition of pictured objects, for he will sometimes, on demand, pat or point to the ball, the cup, the doggy, or other familiar objects.

During this period of the child's growth, he may have developed the following concepts relating to books:

Book as an object: Books contain pages to be turned. Books which survive destruction may become well-loved objects.

Content of book: Pictures resemble familiar objects. Pictures are identified in response to adult naming, although a few fifteen-month-old infants will name pictures if they have the oral vocabulary to do so.

Printed symbols: No notice is given to printing.

From fifteen months to eighteen months

By fifteen months, children usually can say and use with meaning several recognizable words. They understand much more than they can say, as shown by their increasing response to the language that they hear. Many fifteen-month-old children can perform a commission such as, "Give the book to Daddy," "Go and find your teddy," or "Put this in the wastebasket." Parents often report, "He understands everything we say, but he just doesn't seem to be ready to say it himself yet."

Comprehension of heard language patterns precedes articulation of the same patterns by weeks or even months. Vocabulary studies of young children give widely different results, depending on the method of counting words. When words that can be found only in the child's oral speech are counted, eighteen-month-old children usually have a limited vocabulary of about a dozen words, but if "words understood" are counted, the same children may have a large vocabulary and be at a stage of very rapid growth in vocabulary.

Great strides in book activities are made by the child of this age who is provided with books in his environment. Spontaneous oral language is now used with the pictures, and the pictures help to increase vocabulary. At this stage of growth, an infant likes to crawl up on the lap of an adult with a book or magazine and to have the adult say, "Show me the kitty" and "Where's the duck," letting the infant point. Then, reversing the procedure, he likes the adult to point to a picture, asking "What's this?" and letting the infant do the naming. The eighteen-month-old child likes a picture-dictionary that contains many little pictures on every page. Books become an avenue of information, and the child seizes upon them as he does on every other opportunity for finding out about the world. He learns to name a pictured tiger or giraffe (animals he has never really seen), and he astonishes his parents later by naming them correctly when the family takes a trip to the zoo.

At this stage, the child goes beyond the simple naming of pictures and may answer questions about them. To "What is the baby doing?" he may reply with a verb, "Eating." Also, he not only applies to the picture the name of an animal but often gives the animal noises, "bow-wow" or "moo-moo," while looking at the pictures. He enjoys the repetition of these sounds and may "read" an animal book by himself by making appropriate noises for each picture.

The child also begins to notice orientation of pictures. Although he may crawl around on the floor to the opposite side of a book in order to look at a picture right-side-up, he seldom turns the book around.

If books have been regularly in his environment, the

child may have developed the following concepts by the time he is eighteen months:

Book as an object: Books are to be taken care of. Tearing is usually due to lack of motor control.

Content of book: Pictures represent objects both familiar and unfamiliar. Pictures of unfamiliar objects arouse curiosity. A few children begin to notice that pictures have a top and a bottom. Pictures of familiar objects are named spontaneously. Pictures of unfamiliar objects are noticed and serve as a means of vocabulary building. Pictures are interpreted in a very simple way in terms of action or in terms of the sound the object makes. For example, a child may say "z-z-z" while looking at a picture of an airplane or "bye-bye" while looking at a picture of a stroller.

Printed symbols: Very rarely is notice given to printing.

From eighteen months to twenty-four months

Between eighteen and twenty-four months, the child adds several words a day to his vocabulary, and at the end of this period he is usually able to understand and speak about 200 words and to understand many more.

Depending upon his experiences up to this point, the two-year-old may have begun to call the process of looking at books "reading." If there is an adult around who takes time to look at books with him, he will enjoy the activity. He continues to build his vocabulary by learning the names of unknown objects in pictures. He becomes aware that pictures can do more than just resemble objects. He wants to have something happen in each picture and begins to listen to a story read or told by the adult while looking at a sequence of related pictures. He likes repetition rather than plot, with the action in each picture repeated but with a different character performing the action: "A dog said, 'Bow-wow, I want something to eat,' A kitty said, 'Mew-mew, I want something to eat,' " and ending with a climax of "A baby said, 'Mommy, Mommy, I want something to eat.' " Or he likes to have the same character in each picture doing various acts, such as "Billy got up," "He washed his face," "He combed his hair," "He put on his clothes," "He ate his breakfast." If the two-year-old's own name can be substituted for the name of the child in the book, the story goes especially well.

At this stage, the child prefers to have a book read and reread until he masters the vocabulary and sentence patterns. He becomes confused if too many new books are given to him at one time. Often the first reading of a book presents the child with new language forms that are meaningless but that gradually take on meaning as he studies the pictures and listens to the language patterns repeated again and again.

The child who has been given a variety of experiences with books may have developed the following book concepts by the time he is two:

Book as an object: The child continues to develop concepts of good care of books (if care of books is taught him). He turns pages carefully and does not tear them. He realizes that the book has a front and back.

Content of book: Pictures have a top and a bottom. Pictures do more than represent objects; they suggest action and events taking place in sequence—they tell a story. Adults tell stories about the pictures. The same language is used with reference to each picture. The events portrayed by pictures are continuous from one picture to the next. The process of looking at books is called "reading."

Printed symbols: Two-year-olds begin to show an awareness of print—they notice that there is something else on a page besides the pictures.

From two years to six years: a pattern of language growth

The child's language growth, which is substantial throughout the early years, continues with no apparent deceleration in this period from two to six. His vocabulary continues to grow, he develops facility with the syntax of the language he hears at home, and he improves his articulation of the speech sounds of that language.

Vocabulary development: the two types of vocabulary. The child's oral vocabulary is of two types: (1) the words he knows well enough to use himself in his own speech *(the vocabulary of use)* and (2) the words he understands when he hears them but which he does not himself attempt to use. This latter vocabulary, which includes of course all the words that he himself uses, is considerably larger at any given age than the vocabulary of use. It is frequently referred to as *the vocabulary of recognition.*

The vocabulary of recognition. A frequently quoted study of the vocabulary of recognition[1] indicates that the average six-year-old child knows the meanings of approximately 23,700 words, with a range from 6000 words to 48,000 words, or a difference in vocabulary size from smallest to largest in the neighborhood of 42,000 words.

A later study[2] indicates a median vocabulary of 13,000 words for a six-year-old child, with a difference in vocabulary size from smallest to largest in the neighborhood of 13,000 words.

The figures just quoted are sometimes mistakenly referred to as an indication of the number of words a child is prepared to use in his own speech. Such is not the case. These figures represent only an estimate of the total number of words (and derivative words) to which a child is able to respond in some meaningful way.

The vocabulary of use. The number of words a child can use to express himself is in all cases much smaller than the vocabulary to which he can respond. Estimates of the vocabulary of use vary. A recent study of the speaking vocabulary of kindergarten children[3] estimates a vocabulary of 3728 words. This finding may be compared with a much earlier, but still widely quoted, count of the speaking

[1] Mary Katherine Smith, "Measurement of the Size of General English Vocabulary Through the Elementary Grades and High School," *Genetic Psychology Monographs*, vol. 24 (1941), pp. 311-345.
[2] Mildred C. Templin, *Certain Language Skills in Children: Their Development and Interrelationships.* Minneapolis: University of Minnesota Press, 1957.
[3] Clifford John Kolson, "The Vocabulary of Kindergarten Children." University of Pittsburgh, 1960. (Unpublished Doctoral Dissertation)

vocabulary of kindergarten children—that of the International Kindergarten Union, prepared in 1928.[4] The IKU study indicated a speaking vocabulary of around 2596 words, or 1132 fewer than the number found by Dr. C. J. Kolson. Expressed as a per cent, the 1960 count represents an increase over the 1928 count of 44 per cent. Some reading authorities view even the Kolson estimate as minimal for today's children.

The effects of television on the vocabulary of preschool children. The question of how television affects a child's language development is less easily answered than are questions relating to other factors affecting language growth which have been systematically studied over a relatively long period of time. Television is relatively new to the American scene, and it achieved its extraordinary degree of popularity in a phenomenally short period of time. As a result, an unusual situation in adult-child understanding developed: *Adults who grew up in a world that never even heard of television were planning and directing instruction for children who never knew a world without TV.*

As a result of this wide gap between the experiences of the two generations, it may be that the people who have explored the phenomenon of television and its impact on children growing up under its influence have not themselves been sufficiently aware of the extent of change that TV made in the environment of the preschool child.

There have been numerous studies of the amount of time children spend in front of the TV set and of the programs they prefer. There have also been studies of television's psychological effects—for example, of the effect of violence in TV programs on children's aggressive behavior or the effect on youngsters of early exposure to adult mores in dating and marriage. These may be problems to which adults tend for one reason or another to be sensitive.

The effect of television on language development, on the

---

[4] International Kindergarten Union, *A Study of the Vocabulary of Children Before Entering First Grade*. Baltimore: Williams and Wilkins, 1928.

other hand, has received very little attention. One team of researchers has recently made a study of the effects of TV on preschool children's vocabulary,[5] but it is still too early to determine what impact their findings may have on instructional procedures. Hypothesizing that massive exposure to this new communications medium, especially during the preschool years, would have some effect on language development, these investigators designed an experiment that would enable them to compare the vocabulary of first-grade children who had lived with TV with the vocabulary of children who had never experienced television.

The study found that, in general, children who had been viewing television came into first grade prepared to "get off to a faster start" than children who had not had television experiences. The amount of advantage accruing to the child through TV exposure seemed to depend on his level of intelligence. Children at both ends of the intelligence scale—the high group and the low group—who had been living with television had acquired a vocabulary about one year beyond that of the children of comparable intelligence who had not had television experiences. The middle-intelligence group was less noticeably affected, although amount of viewing was a significant factor with these children also. Children of middle intelligence who had been heavy viewers of television came into first grade with significantly larger vocabularies than children of the same intelligence group who did not watch TV often.

In subsequent years of school, according to the same study, the vocabulary gains of the television users fade out. The vocabulary of sixth-grade children showed no relationship to television experiences, nor did that of tenth-grade children.

The researchers concluded that while TV contributes substantially to a fast start in learning, the advantage does not last. Television aids vocabulary growth most during the preschool years. Two explanations of this phenomenon

[5] Wilbur Schramm, Jack Lyle, and Edwin B. Parker, *Television in the Lives of Our Children*. Stanford, Calif.: Stanford University Press, 1961.

are suggested: (1) The preschool or first-grade child has not yet learned to read well enough to use print as a source of word knowledge and information, and (2) the incidental learning from television is of less value in the years beyond first grade because of the repetitiveness of the programs and because of the low intellectual level of the programs that most children choose to watch.

Research about the syntax of the preschool child. Two factors of children's speech that have been studied relate to their growing competence with the structure of the language. These factors are the average length of sentence used and what may be referred to as grammatical accuracy.

Average sentence length. The average length of sentence used by the child increases steadily during the two-to-six-year period and appears to have increased at all age levels during the last two decades. An early study[6] completed during the 1930's indicated that the average length of sentence used by a three-year-old child was 3.4 words, while the five-and-a-half-year-old used sentences averaging 4.4 words in length.

A later study[7] published in 1957 indicated that children are now using longer sentences at each comparable age level. As in the case of vocabulary, this is probably the result of the greatly increased opportunities for hearing language on radio and television, although no research specifically relating TV to sentence length has been reported. Mildred Templin's figures show that a three-year-old child uses sentences averaging 4.1 words; the five-year-old uses sentences averaging 5.7 words; and the six-year-old uses sentences averaging 6.6 words. There is sound evidence to indicate that today's six-year-old has acquired a skill with language, especially in building sentences, which is greater than that of the nine-year-old of twenty years ago.

[6] Dorothea McCarthy, "Language Development in Children," in *Manual of Child Psychology*, Leonard Carmichael, editor. New York: John Wiley and Sons, Inc., 1954.
[7] Mildred C. Templin, *op. cit.*

Readers who are particularly interested in this aspect of trends in language readiness may be interested in the table below, which shows the findings from highly comparable studies made in the 1930's and in the 1950's.

Children are using longer sentences
How sentence length has increased since the 1930's

Age of children studied	Average number of words per sentence in children's spoken language	
	1930-1937[8]	1957[9]
3	3.4	4.1
3½	4.3	4.7
4	4.4	5.4
4½	4.6	5.4
5	—	5.7
5½	4.4	—
6	—	6.6
6½	5.0	—
7	—	7.3
8	—	7.6
9	6.5	—

Grammatical accuracy. There is no real change with age in respect to the parts of speech used in expressive language. The use of the various parts of speech seems to be largely determined by the structure of the language. By three years of age, most children have learned to conform to the demands of the structure of their mother tongue.[10]

[8] Ages 3, 3½, 4, 4½, from Dorothea McCarthy, "Language Development in Children," *op. cit.*, p. 546. Ages 5½, 6½, 9. *Ibid.*, p. 547.
[9] All ages, from Mildred Templin, *op. cit.*, p. 79, Table 39.
[10] Mildred Templin, *op. cit.*

As for correctness of speech, a three-year-old is about two-thirds as accurate grammatically as an eight-year-old. Only the degree of complexity of the grammatical constructions appears to increase steadily with the child's age.[11]

Articulation. Articulation also improves with age. The most marked improvement in accuracy of articulation takes place between two and three years of age, but development beyond the age of three is quite steady to about eight years of age. Most children of eight have mastered the speech sounds of their language. The consonant elements, especially the double- and triple-consonant blends, are mastered more slowly than the vowel elements. Indicated in per cent of sounds correctly articulated, the progress from two to six is about as follows: The child of two articulates about 32 per cent of the sounds of English correctly; the child of three, about 60 per cent; the child of four, about 77 per cent; the child of five, about 88 per cent; and the child of six, about 89 per cent.[12] In general, the sounds the child uses most frequently in his own everyday speech are those with which he shows the greatest ability in articulation.

Development in relation to printed materials. Those children who have access to books change in their book behavior between the years of two and six. They become aware that books have titles; they begin to develop an awareness of the front of the book, as distinguished from the back; and they probably begin to adjust the book so that the pictures are right side up.

At two and one-half years. At two and one-half the pictures and stories become very real to the child. He may kiss the baby, slap the villain, or express his sympathy in such words as "Poor Jack and Jill fell down—don't cry." He will talk to pictured characters and, if his normal social

[11] *Ibid.*
[12] Dorothea McCarthy, "Language Development in Children," *op. cit.*, p. 537.

contacts are limited, he may create an imaginary playmate out of a book character.

The child at this age, if he has an opportunity, will pay increasing attention to the oral language which accompanies the pictures. If an adult reads to him he will tend to memorize verbatim from frequent repetition of the stories. He will become increasingly aware of the top and bottom of the picture and may even adjust a book so that the picture will be right side up for another person.

Alphabet books, if received, are appreciated for their colors rather than for the alphabet. A few children of two and one-half may notice large printed letters, but most children of this age ignore letter names even in alphabet books.

Depending on the amount and kind of experience which a child may have had with books, the following concepts may have been developed by the age of two and one-half:

Book as an object: Books are to be put away after use. Books are decorated with color.

Content of the book: Pictured characters often seem as real as actual people. The events pictured or told about can make one feel happy or sad or angry. Books give information one needs to know about things like trains and airplanes. The language adults use in reading books is constant for each page or picture. This language can be remembered and retold to one's self, especially if the language contains catchy sounds and jingles and is very simple and repetitive.

Printed symbols: Some children may notice the capital letters in alphabet books, but they rarely attempt to name them.

From three years to six years: other growth in book behavior. The growth of a child's book behavior from three to six years becomes increasingly difficult to generalize. The child who attends nursery school at age three will extend his book experiences by sitting around with a group of other children listening while the teacher reads a story and shows the pictures. If the child has an opportunity to hear stories at home, he may dramatize the stories and jingles, particularly if an adult suggests the actions to him.

Many children of this age, however, do not attend nursery school, and many mothers do not have time to sit and read. If the child does have some of these listening experiences, he will learn to tolerate longer language content with each picture and will even listen to an occasional passage which has no accompanying picture. This is a distinct gain over the younger child, who can hear only a brief sentence or two before turning the page to see the next picture.

Under optimum conditions for listening to stories, either at home or at nursery school or both, the three-year-old will develop rapidly in ability to interpret pictures and stories. He may make spontaneous comments that show anticipation of outcome and simple reasoning. He may develop enough language to describe as well as identify objects in pictures, as "nice little kitty." Some three-year-old children can retell a simple story of three episodes, if the episodes are well linked and if the lead into the second or third episode is very evident in the pictures. In some cases an adult may help by giving a clue to each succeeding episode.

Children who have developed considerable interest in books at three years may learn to name four or five capital letters in their alphabet books. Usually a letter in the child's name will be learned, together with O, S, or other letters having a distinctive appearance. Children whose book interests are not developed may continue to ignore the printed symbols in books, giving attention chiefly to the pictures and stories as told by adults. Regardless of intelligence level, children who have had no experiences with books will have developed virtually no book skills or book concepts.

At four years, the child who has been exposed to books may have learned to distinguish between reality and fantasy and will probably prefer books that are definitely one or the other. He enjoys humorous pictures, silly language in stories, and nonsense rhymes. He enjoys looking at books and hearing stories read in groups of children, if he has an opportunity to become accustomed to this experience. He may pore over books alone if he cannot find someone to play with. He is able to memorize stories and, if an available and attentive adult responds, he will insist on having stories reread verbatim. In such instances, he may correct an adult who substitutes a word or condenses the content of a familiar paragraph into a sentence.

Many of the four-year-old's questions relate to "Why?" or "What for?" He wants explanations of everything that he sees or hears; a picture or story may result in many questions and his own interpretations. Thus, instead of interrupting the reader to go on to the next picture or episode, the child himself may sometimes now need to be interrupted so that a book may be finished in a reasonable time.

Children of four and five with a background of book experience begin to realize that there is a relationship between the printed text and the story. They begin to understand that the reader is getting his cues as to what to say from the text. They may refer to the printed text as "some reading"—for example, "There's some reading on this box." They may also distinguish printed text from handwritten text which children of this age sometimes refer to as "writing." Some four- and five-year-olds may try to "write" by drawing crude letter forms, often reversing or inverting the forms. In most instances, they are not aware of printed words within a text but will select letters here and there to copy. Usually capital letters stand out prominently in a text and are chosen for reproduction. The capital letter forms are, in most cases, more impressive to the child than the small-letter forms. A few children at four or five learn to identify some of the letters by name.

Under optimum conditions, including ample access to children's books and a continuity of experience in listening to stories, the following book concepts may be developed by the time the child enters school:

Book as an object: Concepts of book care are extended. The tendency to mark in books is decreasing.

Content of the book: The language value of books now comes to the foreground and begins to rival the picture to some extent, especially if the child has good verbal ability. Pictures and stories stimulate an abundant flow of ideas and expression from the child, usually of the "why" or explanatory type. The child likes to have a clear distinction made between fantasy and reality, since he is still not too sure of the difference himself. Language used in books is often memorized and repeated.

Printed symbols: The child begins to recognize that the printed text tells the reader what to say. Printing is differentiated roughly from writing. Little notice is taken of the orientation of a letter. Letters are frequently drawn or copied in reverse as well as in correct orientation.

THE CHILD AND HIS LANGUAGE COME TO SCHOOL

The preceding paragraphs have described briefly the language development of children until the time of school entry. An attempt has been made to describe what is generally viewed as typical behavior of the majority of children at successive stages of growth. In the case of book behavior, the successive age levels described represent typical behavior under the indicated environmental conditions. No description given, however, should be viewed unconditionally as the description of any individual child. Each child is unique, an individual conforming to no "typical" pattern of growth—conforming, in fact, to no pattern but his own. Meanwhile, the experiences that grow out of the limits and the advantages of his own particular environment become day by day more deeply integrated into his own intellectual and social growth. His language develops as an imitation of the language he hears. His book behavior develops in response to the book behavior of the adults who surround him. If there are no books at home the child will learn little about books. If Spanish is spoken at home rather than English, the child will learn Spanish. Along with these environmental factors, individual differences of all kinds will already have interacted with the influences of background and early experience.

The teacher of beginning reading can be sure that her group will include boys and girls of just about every level of linguistic development and that not one of them will conform completely to any rigorously outlined growth pattern. She must become acquainted with each individual boy and girl in her class and learn especially the particular level of linguistic ability which has been reached by each. Only when she knows this can she *start where they are* in leading them from their oral language skills into the skills of understanding printed language.

The following chapter describes a plan which the classroom teacher may use during the first few weeks of school to obtain important basic information about the individual language profile of each boy and girl in her room.

BIBLIOGRAPHY

Hymes, James L., Jr. *Before the Child Reads.* Evanston, Illinois: Row, Peterson and Co., 1958. Discusses preparation for reading with emphasis on the needs of five- and six-year-olds for a great variety of experiences, both direct and vicarious.

International Kindergarten Union. *A Study of the Vocabulary of Children Before Entering First Grade.* Baltimore: Williams and Wilkins, 1928. A milestone in the history of vocabulary studies. An analysis of the oral vocabularies of preschool children as recorded by parents and kindergarten teachers.

Kolson, Clifford John. *The Vocabulary of Kindergarten Children.* Unpublished Ph.D. dissertation, University of Pittsburgh, 1960. A measure of the speaking vocabulary of kindergarten children in 1960. Includes a comparison with the words found in the International Kindergarten Union list (1928).

McCarthy, Dorothea. "Language Development in Children," *Manual of Child Psychology*, ed. Leonard Carmichael. New York: John Wiley and Sons, Inc., 1954. Extensive review of research relating to language development in children. Includes bibliography of 773 items.

Millard, Cecil V., and Rothney, John W. M. *The Elementary School Child.* New York: Dryden Press, 1957. Case materials for the study of social and intellectual development during the elementary school years.

Schramm, Wilbur; Lyle, Jack; and Parker, Edwin B. *Television in the Lives of Our Children*. Stanford, California: Stanford University Press, 1961. Reports of research relating to the use of television in ten communities in the United States and Canada. Includes studies of how children use television, what they learn from television, and social and psychological effects of television.

Smith, Mary Katherine. "Measurement of the Size of General English Vocabulary Through the Elementary Grades and High School," *Genetic Psychology Monographs*, 24 (1941) 311-345. A study designed to determine the total number of words "which had any significant meaning for the child." Children in Grades One, Two, and Three were examined individually; children in Grade Four and above were tested in progressively larger groups.

Templin, Mildred C. *Certain Language Skills in Children: Their Development and Interrelationships*. Minneapolis, The University of Minnesota Press, 1957. Provides normative measures of articulation of speech sounds, sound discrimination, sentence structure, and vocabulary.

chapter two

Teacher Meets Pupil

The preceding chapter described the ways in which the child develops his linguistic ability and his "book behavior" in the period from birth to school entrance. If each child followed precisely this growth pattern, the teacher of beginning reading would find life much simpler. She would need just one master plan for teaching reading, since one plan would suit all pupils and no individual adjustments would be needed.

Actually no human being conforms exactly to the pattern. Children come in an infinite variety of shapes, sizes, and patterns. Each classroom contains as many growth patterns as there are pupils in it. Each child follows the general pattern in some respects, but in his special combination of characteristics he is himself and no one else.

Thus, one of the biggest problems confronting the teacher of beginning reading is the problem of getting acquainted:

getting to know each child as he is. The child's language constitutes one of the most important avenues through which the teacher can learn about him. It is chiefly through language that she becomes acquainted with his mind. She may infer what he is thinking or feeling from his play activities, but his actual formulation of thoughts and feelings in language is a major step toward clarification of ideas and mutual understanding.

THE IMPORTANCE OF EVALUATING LANGUAGE ABILITY

Even more important to the teacher of beginning reading is the fact that oral language skill is the basis of learning to read. Thus, early recognition of the various levels of language ability possessed by the pupils in her class gives the teacher the necessary basis for planning her total language-arts and pre-reading program.

How best to obtain this early recognition of the levels of ability and the nature of the ability of the pupils in her class is one of the first and most persistent problems that confront the teacher of beginning reading. She may, of course, use some of the reading-readiness tests that are available. These are described in some detail in Chapter 8. But during the first days of school, she needs a more personal contact with the language background of each of her pupils. She needs to know specifically how each child uses language in expressing his own ideas. Tests investigate a child's ability to understand language, but, at beginning levels, they may not tell the teacher all she wants to know about how the child is able to use language. The teacher needs to hear the child use language himself, to hear him expressing his own ideas in his own words. In this way she learns what words he can use, what concepts he attaches to them, how he puts words together, what kinds of ideas he tries to express, and how successfully he is able to express them. She discovers whether his vocabulary and syntax are predominantly English, or Spanish, or German, or a particular dialect of English.

Alert teachers working daily with young children develop a remarkable sensitivity to the language background and potential of each pupil. But even experienced teachers frequently find it difficult to identify and describe the specific strands or aspects of language skill which together make up the individual child's language power. Since this is a dilemma confronted by many teachers, the following plan for describing and rating language power in self-expression is presented.

A classification of oral language skills

Clinical psychologists, working with speech and language specialists, have identified certain characteristics of speech (oral language) which seem most useful in describing the individual child's expressive language skills. Two of these characteristics, the quality of the child's ideas and the way in which he is able to define words, are primarily aspects of the child's thinking, as revealed through his speech. Two other characteristics are aspects of expressive language: the way the child verbalizes his ideas and the quality of his sentence structure (syntax). This classification of the child's oral language skills may be briefly restated as follows:

1. How a child thinks, as revealed by the quality of his ideas.
2. How a child thinks, as revealed by the nature of his definitions of words.
3. How a child uses words, as revealed by his ability to verbalize ideas.
4. How a child uses words, as revealed by his command of sentence structure.

A clinical approach to analysis of oral language

The best methods of analyzing the child's oral language depend to a large degree on the facilities available to the classroom teacher. In a clinical setting where a child may be individually examined, the procedure for studying these aspects of a child's language might be as follows.

A carefully selected picture[1] is to be presented privately to each child, who is encouraged by the clinician to "tell all about it." The clinician or teacher then records verbatim, possibly on tape, everything the child says, occasionally encouraging him with such nondirecting phrases as "That's fine. Tell me some more." The child's entire verbal output is subsequently analyzed in relation to idea quality, ability to verbalize ideas, sentence structure, and use of voice and articulatory mechanism. The child's ability to define words is explored by means of a vocabulary "test," presented orally by such questions as "Tell me what a ball is," or, if the child is unable to reply, "Find one in the picture." All responses are to be recorded verbatim and analyzed.

The procedure just described may be used by the classroom teacher if she has time and if the physical classroom facilities permit testing each child individually. Many classroom teachers, however, find such individual testing difficult when they are simultaneously responsible for the entire class. The following variation of the clinical approach is suggested as a device which the classroom teacher may find easier to use.

A classroom approach to analysis of oral language

Just because the classroom teacher has the responsibility for thirty or more boys and girls simultaneously instead of just one, she need not feel that she is necessarily at a disadvantage in the task of analyzing oral language. She has, in fact, one substantial advantage over the clinician: she is with the children all the time instead of being limited to one short exposure, which is usually the case in the clinical situation.

---

[1] A picture would be selected to satisfy these criteria: (1) There should be two or more easily recognized characters in the picture, such as boy, girl, baby, mother, father, or pets. (2) There should be a central activity or "story," such as playing a game, having a picnic, making cookies, or getting ready for bed. (3) Each character should be doing something different. (4) The setting or background should be appropriate enough to indicate where the action is taking place but should not contain so many items as to distract from the main theme.

For purposes of analyzing oral language this constant contact can be turned to good use. Instead of observing and analyzing the child's responses to one particular picture, the teacher may observe daily the oral language of her pupils in all kinds of situations. This observation should include not only formal classroom discussions or recitations but also informal situations outside of class, before or after school, as she hears or overhears snatches of conversation, or at recess or morning milk-break.

A PLAN FOR RECORDING A CHILD'S USE OF LANGUAGE

Every teacher of young children has long since discovered that observation of language can be a rich source of information about the language background and language abilities and disabilities of her pupils. What she needs in most cases is a systematic and simple means of recording, describing, analyzing, and, where desirable, rating such language behavior.

The following pages present scales and descriptive materials to help the teacher keep such a record. There is a rating scale for each of the four areas classified earlier in this chapter: (1) quality of ideas, p. 30; (2) definition of words, p. 33; (3) ability to verbalize ideas, p. 36; and (4) mastery of sentence structure, p. 38. Each of these scales has five levels, ranging from Level 1, the lowest, up to Level 5, the highest. In most cases more than five levels cannot be easily discriminated by means of subjective judgment. Some teachers may even want to reduce the five levels to three, dropping Levels 2 and 4 and identifying pupils only as "below average," "average," or "above average" in each of the specified characteristics.

Information as to how a child defines words may not be as readily obtained as some of the other types of information. However, many classroom discussions involve questions of definition, and the teacher may find that questions starting "What is a . . ." occur more frequently during the teaching day than she had realized.

All the teacher needs as equipment for making use of

Rating chart for four aspects of oral language

Pupil	Quality of ideas	Definition of words	Ability to verbalize ideas	Mastery of sentence structure
George	3	3	4	4
Susan	2	2	3	2
Timothy	2	3	2	2

the scales is a chart. This she can easily prepare by listing pupils' names at the left of a long sheet of paper (or several sheets in a notebook) and the four areas for observation across the top. The diagram above suggests how such a chart might look when a few ratings and descriptions have been entered.

Discovering how a child thinks

The thinking process is a highly individual thing and essentially private. The outcomes of the thinking may be revealed in a variety of ways, but the actual thinking process can be inferred only from what appear to be the results.

Two aspects of expressive language may be considered by teachers who seek some indication of the level and nature of their pupils' thinking: the quality of the child's ideas and the way the child "defines" words. These two observable behaviors have therefore been selected as bases for the scales which follow. Each area is given in the order in which it appears in the chart above.

Quality of ideas. Small children at approximately the beginning reading level may exhibit a wide range of quality in their ideas. Some children appear to limit themselves almost entirely to the here and now, the concrete, and the individual object or event. Other children may notice some kind of relationship among objects or events, or indicate some thinking about things not in the immediate environment. Still others may demonstrate ideas that indicate an awareness of cause and effect or of time sequence. Some children may perceive separate objects or events as comprising a total situation from which they may state a main idea, draw a "moral," make a generalization, or make a summarizing statement.

The quality of a child's idea is often judged on the basis of his use of language; "adult" or "correct" English idioms are often equated with maturity of thinking. Actually the language structures used by a six-year-old child are a reflection of the language the child has heard, and thus it may or may not be an accurate indication of the level of his thinking. A child, for example, may not use "because" as a conjunction in a fully verbalized, dependent-clause-plus-independent-clause sentence. He may nevertheless be perfectly clear in his own mind about the cause-and-effect relation of one event to another. An adult trying to appraise this child's thinking should attempt to recognize the child's manner of indicating his awareness of a cause-and-effect relationship. The relation between quality of idea and sentence structure is discussed further on pages 37-39.

The scale given below, designed to indicate to the teacher five varying levels of idea quality that she may find among members of her class, has been phrased so as to refer as little as possible to syntactical structures and as much as possible to the quality of the ideas themselves, independent of the structure in which they are embedded.

Suggested scale for quality of ideas

1. Ideas fully concrete. Concerned with the immediate environment. Objects and events seen as separate items. Not concerned with relationships.

Example (response to a picture showing a dog jumping up to snatch an ice-cream cone from a baby's hand):

> "It's about a baby and a dog and an ice-cream cone."

2. Sees some objects and events in relation to each other. Relationships seen are concerned with the concrete and the here and now. Characters are related to their actions.

   Examples (picture as described above):

   > "The baby's crying."
   > "The dog's jumping up."
   > "The baby's eating."

3. Sees relationships between objects and events, including relationships of size, shape, color, use, distance, and cause and effect. Begins to include in his ideas some people, things, or events farther away in time or space. Recognizes simple emotional reactions and motives of characters. Forms sensory images (visual, auditory, thermal, tactile, kinesthetic).

   Examples (picture as described above):

   > "It's a hot day."
   > "The baby wants the dog to go away."
   > "Somebody gave the baby an ice-cream cone."
   > "The baby's scared."

4. Sees relationships of various kinds as Level 3 but tends to include the more abstract qualities as well as the concrete and immediate. Anticipates events, deduces more complex cause-and-effect relationships and time relationships. Recognizes simple character traits.

Example (picture as described above):

> "The dog wants to get the baby's cone. I think he's going to get it, too. He's a bad dog."

5. Ideas as at Level 4 but with the addition of some evaluation and judgment. Generalizes within the limits of his experience. Makes judgments which include the consideration of abstract concepts.

Examples (picture as described above):

> "People shouldn't give babies cones when dogs are around."
> "Pets are sometimes a nuisance."
> "Dogs don't know any better."

Definition of words. The process of defining a word is not so simple as people sometimes suppose. Many adults give painfully inadequate or confused responses when asked to define a word they themselves have used. They murmur something like, "Oh, you know, the _____ (repeating the word they are trying to define). You know what I'm trying to say."

Children, too, find verbal definitions difficult. What is generally viewed as a "good" definition, by adult standards, requires a fair degree of abstract thinking plus a background of related concepts which permit adequate classification and accurate description. The child who can describe a dog as a "pet," for example, knows not only what a dog is but also what a variety of other household pets are. In addition, he has grasped the generic concept, knows the term *pet*, and is able to identify the word *dog* as a member of this class. Thus, the nature of a definition of a word is a highly useful clue in judging the quality of a child's (or an adult's) thinking.

The scale of five levels of definition which is given on the next page includes examples of definitions of two words: *ball* and *window*.

Suggested scale for definition of words

1. Cannot verbalize any definition. (May be able to respond to the word by pointing to the object or to a picture of the object.)

2. Repeats the name of the object or uses the name of the object in a sentence.

    Examples: "A ball is a ball."
    "I got a ball."
    "A window is . . . well, it's a window."

3. Defines by stating the use of the object (or shows its use with pantomime).

    Examples: "A ball is to play with."
    "A window is to see out of."

4. Defines by describing.

    Examples: "A ball is round and big and made out of rubber."
    "A window is clear-like and has window-panes."

5. Defines by classifying or by classifying plus describing. May recognize variant meanings.

    Examples: "A ball is a kind of toy, and there's a ball where you dance."
    "A window is something glass over a hole in the wall."

Discovering how a child uses words

A child's use of language in expressing his own thoughts reveals much about his language background and how well that background is suited to the task of learning to read.

The differences among six-year-olds in expressive language may be as great as the differences in our society as a whole.

The child who comes from a family of adults who are relatively well educated and verbally facile may be far advanced in his use of the spoken word. He will have learned to imitate many of the idioms and speech habits of academically trained adults. His ideas, of whatever level, will appear relatively mature because they are expressed in relatively mature form.

Less fortunate children come to school with meager experience in language. They know relatively few words and some of those they do know may not be permitted in the classroom. Other children may not have heard English spoken at home, or they may have been exposed to any one of a variety of substandard dialects of English.

The level of language usage may or may not represent the level of the child's ideas. A child with high-level verbal facility may not have any more mature ideas than the child whose language is inadequate or unacceptable. The following example demonstrates how language facility may be almost irrelevant to the quality of the ideas being expressed.

Two children are confronted with the same picture and asked to respond to it. The picture shows a dog jumping up to snatch an ice-cream cone from a baby's hand. One child responds: "Dog gonna get cone. Bad dog!" The other says, "The dog who is jumping up on the baby wants to get the baby's cone. If he does get it, I think that dog should be spanked." The first child used six words plus gestures. The second child demonstrated adult competence with syntax, creating two somewhat long and grammatically correct sentences. One might argue as to which child in this instance expressed himself more effectively. But there can be little doubt as to which child possessed the kind of language power which provides readiness for the academic task of learning to read.

Language power is not easy to analyze and describe objectively, but two aspects of it are frequently used as bases for such estimates: the ability to verbalize an idea and the quality of the syntax, or sentence structure.

Ability to verbalize ideas. The child's ability to put his thoughts into words depends upon several different language abilities working together, combined with a certain attitude or feeling of wanting to express himself. The language abilities include first of all a vocabulary sufficient to carry the ideas, then enough command of the syntax of the language to be able to put the words together in their proper relationships, plus enough ease or facility in the business of putting words together to be able to produce an amount of language sufficient for the purpose.

All of these skills, abilities, and understandings, working together, may result in successful self-expression, provided still another quality is present in the situation: namely, a feeling of self-confidence and security so that the skills and abilities of language can function normally.

Vocabulary. The difference in vocabulary among six-year-olds is enormous. There is first of all, of course, a difference in size of vocabulary. No exact count is ever possible but, as was indicated in Chapter 1, the number of words a six-year-old child can respond to ranges probably from a minimum of about 6000 words to a maximum of about 48,000. Nor are the words themselves the same for any two children. Words that are everyday experiences for some children may never have been heard by others. The quality of the vocabulary differs. Some children have acquired a large stock of words of the type they will hear in the classroom and learn to read. Other children may know words which the teacher doesn't use and which don't seem to appear in the textbooks.

Sentence structure. The way in which children put words together varies as do the vocabularies, and for similar reasons: the children have been exposed to different kinds of language experiences. Variations of sentence structure are discussed in more detail in the section on sentence structure that follows (pp. 37-39).

Amount of verbal output. The amount of language output needs to be appropriate to the ideas to be expressed. Some children may find putting words together so difficult a chore that they stop talking before they have made clear

what they have in mind. Others may have a seemingly endless patter that confuses rather than clarifies, and is equally
inadequate for the job of self-expression. The child who is
best prepared for the language learning ahead is the child
who has learned to tailor his verbal output to the require-
ments of what he wants to say.

Self-confidence. The feeling of self-confidence necessary
to promote free and natural self-expression in the classroom
can be encouraged or discouraged by the teacher. The
atmosphere of the classroom needs to be not only one of
interest in the individual, emphasis on what each person
has to contribute, care for good verbal expression, but also
tolerance of imperfections. The teacher who is genuinely
interested in what a child has to say will in most cases be
able to make her pupils feel that their ideas are important
and that their contributions to discussions are welcome.

The scale below describes five levels of ability in the
verbalization of ideas.

Suggested scale for ability to verbalize ideas

1. No ideas clearly expressed. Talks very little or far too
   much. Confuses the listener through inappropriate use
   of words or inability to put words together to show
   their relationships. Frequently disorganized or even
   incoherent. May shrug shoulders, point to an object,
   or grimace without verbalizing.

2. Verbal expression of ideas severely limited, but better
   than at Level 1. Words may sometimes not be clearly
   related to one another, or they may be inappropriate
   or incomprehensible, or may be too few to express
   an idea adequately.

3. Moderately clear in verbal expression. May sometimes
   become either blocked or overproductive, and may
   sometimes use words inappropriately, but manages to
   express some of his ideas adequately. May digress from
   his subject.

4. Uses words adequately for clear expression of his ideas. Appears to be able to say what he wants to say, and does not usually talk too much. Stays on the subject; usually avoids irrelevancies.

5. Same as Level 4 but in addition to the ability to express his own ideas shows a desire and an ability to include others in a conversational manner in what he has to say. May, for example, try to exchange ideas with the teacher or with another pupil.

Mastery of sentence structure.   According to linguists, most children—in any culture—have mastered the basic structures of their language by the time they are six. It might seem to follow from this that every six-year-old would be well equipped to proceed with learning reading and the other language arts simply by building on this basic mastery of syntax.

Actually, as many first-grade teachers have discovered, the situation is not quite that simple. A country so large and so diverse as the United States has not merely "a culture" but a large number of subcultures. The language spoken varies according to socioeconomic, ethnic, and linguistic group characteristics, and according to geographical area. The most basic of English language structures are known to most children who have had an English language background. However, children with experience in languages other than English may not have mastered many of the basic English structures, such as word order or the use of definite and indefinite articles. The language the child uses when he comes to school is simply a reflection of the language of the adults and other children with whom he has associated. At this age, regardless of level of intelligence or potential language ability, his language structures cannot be basically different from those he has been hearing.

What this background of sentence structure may mean to the child entering school is perhaps most easily demonstrated with one example. The child says, "I got home my mother was gone." That is the way he says it. There is no period after home, nor is there a comma. There is no pause.

The first part of the sentence is spoken with a rising inflection which continues directly into the second part. The peak of the rising inflection is on the first syllable of "mother." The voice falls during the rest of the sentence. The relationship of the two ideas is clarified by this use of inflection. To the child, this is a good sentence. It says exactly what he means to say. "I got home my mother was gone." That this is basically an English sentence is demonstrated by the fact that any native speaker of the English language is capable of understanding it. It is not, however, a sentence structure that is going to be useful as a basis for language learning in school.

Thus, although children by the age of six have mastered the basic structures of their language, they still have problems, since "their" language may not be the language of the school nor of the community as a whole.

How much the school can do to alter what has been so firmly learned before the age of six is still open to question. However, it is generally agreed that the earlier the change is attempted the more likely it is that some degree of success can be achieved. This indicates the desirability of early recognition of the nature of the problem. The scale below has been prepared to help the teacher evaluate the child's mastery of English language structures.

Suggested scale for mastery of sentence structure

1. Has not mastered English syntax well enough to be understood. (In most cases the result of a non-English home background.)

2. May alter English word order somewhat in the direction of the syntax of another language, or in the direction of a regional or class pattern of English, but uses sufficiently idiomatic English to be understood.

    Examples: "That man I seen him."
    "That man I saw him."

    (The form of the verb may be acceptable or unacceptable. This is not a question of structure, although the usage and structure variations frequently occur together.)

3. Approaches somewhat nearer to standard English sentence structure. Uses large numbers of subject-verb or subject-verb-object sentences strung together with *and*. Frequently doesn't seem able to terminate the *and . . . and . . . and* sentence. Uses *because* in an incomplete sentence in answer to a question.

> *Example:* "Why did you draw a blue horse?"
> "Because I like blue."

Probably will not use a complete complex sentence with a *because* clause.

Shows relationships by running two ideas together rather than by formulating a complex sentence with an appropriate conjunction.

> *Example:* "I read a book my mother gave it to me."
> "I got home my mother was gone."

4. Manages more frequently to make a stop between sentences. Uses a larger proportion of complete sentences.

5. Approaches standard English syntax. Uses standard word order and a greater variety of acceptable word order. Connects related ideas by using appropriate connectors or implied connectors.

> *Examples:* "When I got home, my mother was gone."
> "I read a book my mother gave me."

OBSERVING OTHER ASPECTS OF
LANGUAGE READINESS

If, over a period of a few weeks at the beginning of the school year, the teacher has an opportunity to rate each child in her class in the four areas discussed above—quality of ideas, nature of definitions, ability to verbalize ideas, and command of sentence structure—she will have a good basic knowledge of the degree of language readiness each one brings to school with him. She will know in general about each child (1) how he thinks and (2) how well he is able to use words to express his thoughts.

For fuller understanding of each child, however, she needs still other types of information. Especially useful are the following: some knowledge of the way he uses his voice and articulatory mechanism; some measure of the degree to which he has learned to control hand and eye movements; and some indication as to his eye and hand preference. The following informal analyses may help the teacher to systematize her observation of these characteristics.

How a child uses his voice and articulatory mechanism

Since the earliest work in reading is largely oral and since an understanding of letter-sound relationships depends to some extent on the ability to form sounds correctly, the child's own speech is important.

Pitch, volume, and quality. There are several aspects of speech to be considered. First of all, how does the child use his voice? This is partly a question of volume. Is his voice loud or soft, or just medium? It is partly a question of pitch. Does he place his voice high or low or in the middle range? It is also a question of quality. Does the voice sound nasal, or denasal, or harsh, or sweet?

These three aspects—pitch, volume, and quality—working together make up the voice of the individual. Each voice can be described in relatively nontechnical terms by some indication of one or more of these three aspects. Descriptive words which may be helpful in making such an analysis include the following:

Volume: soft, medium, loud.

Pitch: low, medium, high.

Quality: sweet, thin, tense, metallic, nasal, harsh, breathy, denasal, husky, monotonous, clear, musical.

Substitutions of sounds.   How good is the child's articulation? Substitutions of sounds in articulation may seriously affect a child's ability to use phonetic cues in attacking unknown words in reading. For example, a child who says *tat* for *cat* may later associate the sound of *t* with the letter *c* and thus have difficulty in attacking new words such as *call* and *cap*, misreading them as *tall* and *tap*. The meanings of the words also may be confused, since the meaning of *tall* could be aroused by the printed word *call*, and *cap* could bring to mind a water *tap* or the verb *tap*.

The teacher may want to describe articulatory problems in various ways. For one child the term "infantile" or "baby talk" may be an adequate reminder for the teacher of the kinds of articulatory defects present. In another instance she may want to note the specific sounds and combinations of sounds with which a child has difficulty.

Rhythm and tempo.   Mature speech is smooth and uninterrupted. There is no repetition of sounds or syllables, no undue prolongation of any sound, and no undue muscular tension. The tempo is relatively even, varied in relation to the mood and emotion to be conveyed. Expressions of joy and excitement, for example, will usually be spoken faster than expressions of sorrow or disappointment. In general, the tempo of a person's speech is a facet of his total personality as well as his mood of the moment. The teacher need not be concerned with correcting the tempo of speech unless it is so excessively fast or slow as to interfere with the child's ability to express himself.

Speech problems best treated by a specialist.   In analyzing the child's speech the classroom teacher should not feel that she is responsible for treating any and all difficulties which she may observe. In general, any speech problem which seems to be of organic origin should, if possible, be diagnosed by a specialist. If the school system provides a speech clinician, the teacher has a ready solution to her problem. Teachers who work in school systems where no clinician is available for consultation may find that they can refer a child to the school nurse or doctor or to the child's family doctor. Also, if possible, parents should be urged to consult an ear-nose-throat specialist and submit his report to the school.

The following types of speech problems are not within the province of the classroom teacher:

1. Speech problems resulting from cleft palate.
2. Speech problems resulting from cerebral palsy.
3. Speech problems growing out of deafness.
4. Other voice and articulatory problems that are organic in nature.
5. Stuttering.
6. Speech problems resulting from aphasia.

The teacher *can*, of course, help the child accept the fact of these differences. Wholesome mental hygiene is highly recommended for any speech problem.

Hand control and handedness

Another physical factor important to reading is the question of hand control and handedness. Hand control is important in developing reading readiness because it is largely through hand movements that the perception of left-to-right sequence is developed. Tallying objects with the hand by touching each object while naming or counting them consecutively is a basic pre-reading skill. To put a finger on the picture to be discussed, or on the first picture in a row of objects in a reading-readiness booklet, is one of the frequent directions given to children in the pre-reading period. With his finger held securely on the picture, the child can look up at the teacher for oral comments, wiggle as he likes, and then look back at the book without losing his place. Hand movements help direct eye movements during early training in control of eye movement, as the child moves hand and eyes while looking at each picture in sequence.

Children who have not established a consistent preference for the right hand or the left hand may have some difficulty in learning which side to start from in reading or in other activities requiring left-to-right sequence. A certain amount of ambidexterity is normally present among children of five and six, even though a preference for right or left hand has usually been established. Therefore, it is a good plan to stress directional sequence in the reading-readiness program with children of these ages.

Determining hand preference. An important part of the teacher's task of getting acquainted with each child is the determination of his hand preference. The following informal activities may be used for determining which hand the child prefers:

1. Place a pencil on a table before the seated child, vertically in front of him, point of pencil midway between right and left hands. Observe the hand with which he grasps the pencil.
2. Have him put a dot in each square of a cross section (one-inch squares may be mimeographed for an entire class) and count the number he can mark in one minute (time accurately). Is he among the best or poorest in the class? Does he shift handedness during this performance?
3. Have him repeat the performance with his unpreferred hand. Compare speed and quality with his previous record and with the class. Ambidextrous children are often low in the class in the preferred-hand test, but high in the unpreferred-hand test. The quality of work of two hands is more similar than that of the majority of children.
4. Note hand used in pretending to throw a ball.
5. Note hand used in pretending to thread a needle.
6. Note hand used in pretending to comb hair.
7. Note hand used in pretending to brush teeth.
8. Note hand used in pretending to eat.
9. Note hand used in pointing to an object across the room.

The foregoing tests will show which children are dominantly right- or left-handed, which are somewhat ambidextrous, and which are almost completely ambidextrous. Some individuals remain ambidextrous for life and in some adult activities they may even have an advantage. In activities such as writing, however, the ambidextrous child may be handicapped in developing skill because he shifts from one hand to the other and does not become proficient with either hand. It is a good plan to suggest that he make a choice of hands and then use that hand consistently for that activity. Do not suggest which hand—that is the child's prerogative—but advise him that he will gain better control if he practices always with the same hand.

A teacher needs to know and to adjust to a child's hand preference, but she should not attempt to change it. By the time a child is six years old, attempts to change handedness may upset his whole system of motor coordination and even disturb his space perception.

Children who are left-handed often need reassurance, because they are in the minority and may feel conspicuous in using the left hand. A complimentary remark about left-handed people, especially about some baseball pitcher who is a "southpaw," may help a boy willingly accept his left-handedness. A left-handed child will feel less conspicuous if he is placed at the end, instead of in the middle, of a row of children at the blackboard or at the table. In the end position he is not so likely to bump elbows or jiggle his right-handed neighbor and is not so apt to draw attention to his left-handedness.

Judging skill in hand movement. A child's skill in hand movement, regardless of hand preference, may be determined by informal tests such as the following:

1. How many blocks high can he build a tower of one-inch cubes? Record the number of cubes just before the tower falls. Allow the best of two trials.
2. How rapidly can he do a simple chore such as putting a number of blocks into a box that just fits them? Scatter the blocks in random style and time the child from the instant he touches the first block until the last one is placed. Record the time in seconds.
3. How accurately can he stay on the line in cutting off a strip of paper? Use ruled paper with about

an inch between lines and let each child cut off one strip from a new sheet with a pair of kindergarten scissors.

4. How accurately can he stay within the line when coloring a circle about two inches in diameter? Prepare mimeographed circles for the whole class.

These four simple tests, which can be given at odd moments, will give the teacher a rough measure of each child's hand control in comparison with other members of the class. By using the entire class as a standard, she can discover pupils who are markedly low or high in these abilities. Steadiness, speed, and accuracy are the three motor skills that are desirable assets in reading.

For the child who is slow to develop skill in hand control, an abundance of tools and games requiring accurate muscular control of the hands is helpful. Tools such as hammers, scissors, and punches are good hand developers. Nested cubes, building blocks, picture puzzles, sewing cards, peg boards, and paper dolls to cut are also good equipment for developing hand control. Coloring books and crayons are especially helpful because of the practice they give in handling books as well as the hand control necessary for coloring within a line.

THE IMPORTANCE OF GETTING ACQUAINTED

Getting acquainted with children is not something that can be done suddenly. It may require days or weeks to assemble all the information that is desirable. Testing for handedness and muscular control will require some time, since individual observation is required. Information about language patterns, or ideas, or ability to define a word may need to be assembled slowly—the teacher adding, as the occasion presents itself, some especially noteworthy and significant example of a certain child's speech or verbal thinking. The chart on page 29 provides a convenient way of recording some of these observations. Once completed it can serve as a graphic reminder of the individual differences for which the teacher needs to plan.

BIBLIOGRAPHY

American Council on Education, Commission on Teacher Education. *Helping Teachers Understand Children*. Washington, D.C.: American Council on Education, 1945. Account of a three-year project in which teachers, psychologists, and sociologists cooperated in a study of child behavior.

Berson, Minnie Perrin. "Individual Differences Among Preschool Children: Four-Year-Olds," *Individualizing Instruction* (NSSE 61st Yearbook, Part I), 112-125. Chicago: National Society for the Study of Education and The University of Chicago Press, 1962. Describes the four-year-old's perception of his world; his intellectual, social, and emotional behavior; and the extent to which a given four-year-old may vary from the "typical" four-year-old.

Breckenridge, Marian Edgar, and Vincent, E. Lee. *Child Development*, 3rd ed. Philadelphia: W. B. Saunders and Co., 1955. Describes the physical and psychological growth of the child, including the influence on growth of home, school, and community; the development of language; and the development of sense perceptions and judgments.

Durkin, Dolores. "A Case-Study Approach Toward an Identification of Factors Associated with Success and Failure in Learning to Read," *California Journal of Educational Research*, 11 (January 1960), 26-33. An exploration of factors associated with success or failure in learning to read. Characteristics associated with failure included a tendency toward shyness or passivity and a lack of self-confidence.

————. "Children Who Read Before Grade One," *The Reading Teacher*, 14 (January 1961), 163-166. Preliminary report of characteristics of 49 children who entered first grade with reading levels from 1.5 up to 4.6.

————. "Children Who Learned to Read at Home," *Elementary School Journal*, 62 (October 1961), 15-18. Follow-up study of 49 pupils who learned to read before entering school. Includes detail on the ways they learned to read.

Gesell, Arnold L, and Ames, Louise B. "The Development of Handedness," *Journal of Genetic Psychology*, 70 (June 1947), 155-175. Study based on periodic observation of a small group of normal infants, with special emphasis on the first year of life. Provides age level summaries of the development of laterality.

Green, Donald Ross, and Simmons, Sadie Vee. "Chronological Age and School Entrance," *Elementary School Journal*, 63 (October 1962), 41-47. Points out the need for more flexibility in instruction in relation to the varying abilities of children entering school.

Hale, Creighton J. "Changing Growth Patterns of the American Child," *Education*, 78 (April 1958), 467-470. A study of the rate of maturation of American children.

Harris, Albert J. "Reading and Human Development," *Development in and Through Reading* (NSSE 60th Yearbook, Part I), 17-34. Chicago: National Society for the Study of Education and The University of Chicago Press, 1961. Discusses various concepts of growth and child development, their relation to the concepts of reading readiness and reading progress. Includes sections on language development, perceptual development, and social-cultural background in relation to reading.

Hildreth, Gertrude. "The Development and Training of Hand Dominance," *Pedagogical Seminar and Journal of Genetic Psychology*, 75 (December 1949), 197-275; 76 (March 1950), 39-144. A review of 258 studies of characteristics of handedness, lateral dominance, and training of handedness.

Morrison, Ida E. "The Relation of Reading Readiness to Certain Language Factors," *Challenge and Experiment in Reading* (International Reading Association Conference Proceedings, Vol. 7, 1962), 119-121. Brief summaries of two studies showing the importance of oral language competence, both speaking and listening, in readiness for reading.

Olson, Willard C. *Child Development*. Boston: D. C. Heath and Company, 1959. Describes the characteristics of broad periods of growth with emphasis on physical development as indicated by height, weight, dentition, development of wrist bones, and grip. Also includes a study of growth curves showing mental age and reading age. Develops the concept of "Organismic age."

Piaget, Jean. *The Language and Thought of the Child*. New York: The Humanities Press, Inc., 1959. (First published in 1926.) Analyses and interpretations of the spontaneous speech of children during their morning activities at the *Institut J. J. Rousseau* in Geneva. The children's remarks were recorded in minute detail in context. The analyses include: functions of language in children at age six; types and stages in the conversation of children between the ages of four and seven; and the questions asked by a child of six.

Sampson, Olive C. "Reading Skill at Eight Years in Relation to Speech and Other Factors," *British Journal of Educational Psychology*, 32 (February 1962), 12-17. Reports the results of a study of the relationship of reading progress to speech development, language growth, socioeconomic level, and emotional adjustment. Pupils were examined before thirty months of age, at five years, and at eight years.

Wheatley, George M., and Hallock, Grace T. *Health Observation of School Children*. New York: McGraw-Hill Book Company, Inc., 1956. Background information to help the teacher understand the health problems of individual pupils.

chapter three

Pupil Meets Print

The early days of the first year in school, before pupils have begun formal reading instruction, are important days for both pupils and teacher. The teacher is engaged in the big job of getting acquainted with each one of her group. She is making some kind of record of their language abilities, perhaps by use of a chart such as that suggested on page 39. Based on the information from such a chart and on all the other knowledge she has of the abilities and problems of each of her pupils, she is working to develop for each of them the basic skills and understandings needed for learning to read.

The pupils, meanwhile, are learning about all sorts of new things and new people and are having all sorts of new experiences. They are finding out what kind of person their teacher is, getting acquainted with each other, and experiencing a grand variety of new sights and sounds and symbols that have not previously played much part in their lives. Many of the new things they do are designated by their teacher as "pre-reading" activities. These activities may range from learning to recognize their own names in print to listening to the teacher read a story or a poem.

To the boys and girls, it seems that there is an endless variety of new things to do. Some of the activities make them look at things very carefully (the teacher calls this "developing visual skills"), some make them listen (the teacher calls this "developing listening skills"), and still others make them do things with their hands, with their feet, with their voices. (These are things the teacher calls "developing oral language skills" and "developing motor skills.") And in addition to all of this, there are books with pictures and sometimes there is writing. The teacher writes the boys' and girls' names, and sometimes she writes other things. This last is something the teacher thinks of as "introducing the conventions of printed English." This is important because through a familiarity with the basic conventions of printed English children begin to see that printed language is just "talk written down."

This chapter will suggest first of all just a few of the devices a teacher may use at the beginning of the year to develop oral language skills, listening skills, visual skills, and skills of interpretation. (More detailed suggestions are offered in later chapters: Chapter 4 presents ways of developing listening skills, Chapter 5 focuses on the development of visual skills, and Chapter 6 emphasizes interpretation.) The major part of this chapter is concerned with ways in which the teacher may approach that most difficult but important task: helping children to understand that *printed language is just talk written down.*

DEVELOPING ORAL LANGUAGE SKILLS AND LISTENING SKILLS

Opportunities for growth in speaking and listening during the pre-reading period are many and various. The first day of school, for example, presents an occasion for encouraging speech and developing desirable speech and language patterns if the teacher chooses to take advantage of it. When she has introduced herself, she can suggest to the boys and girls that they get acquainted with each other. Children may be encouraged to introduce their neighbors or their friends to the rest of the children by using such patterns as, "This is my friend, Holly Green," or simply, "This is Holly." Some may be mature enough to say something like, "This is Holly Green. She lives in my block and we always come to school together."

Other introductions may take place during the first few weeks of school as various persons visit the class. These visitors may include the principal of the school, the school nurse or doctor, or a special area supervisor. In each instance pupils have an opportunity to listen to a good pattern, to assimilate it into their own speech, and, when opportunities arise, to reproduce it in their own introductions. Children whose parents come to school may be invited to introduce their parents to the teacher and to the boys and girls. Additional practice with such language patterns is easily and naturally carried on through the medium of dramatic play. Each such experience provides further practice in both speaking and listening.

Another avenue for practicing both speaking and listening skills is the reporting of experiences. Reporting gives children practice in organizing ideas into acceptable verbal form; in formulating clear, complete sentences; and in listening for the main idea, for the sequence of ideas, and for details. Children may be guided in listening to each other so that any pupil will be ready to summarize a story someone else has told. This procedure helps the child who is telling his story feel that it is important for him to tell it just right. The other boys and girls are encouraged to listen carefully so that they can remember and sum up what the storyteller has said.

Reporting may lead to the learning of new words which some of the children, or even all of them, have not previously had in their vocabularies. A child who has had a vacation by the sea or at a lake may describe the sounds of water. A helpful teacher may suggest ways in which the sounds of waves may be put into words: lapping, splashing, roaring, or booming. Another child may want to tell about the leaves falling. Describing leaves in mid-air is great fun: they sail, they dance, they whirl, they drift. Children themselves will suggest words of remarkable imaginative power. Speaking the words and hearing the words will increase language power as well as listening power and add to boys' and girls' pleasure with language in a wonderful variety of ways.

DEVELOPING VISUAL SKILLS AND INTERPRETATIVE SKILLS

For the beginner, interpreting stories is either interpreting oral language or interpreting picture stories. Both kinds of interpreting get the skill-building program off to a good start. Interpreting oral language develops listening skills, while interpreting picture stories encourages the development of visual skills. Pupils need to learn to respond to nonverbal visual symbols and also to respond to verbal nonvisual symbols. Early practice in the two types of response provides experience of the kind needed later on for reading, namely, responding to verbal visual symbols.

In interpreting a picture story, children first practice habits of careful visual scrutiny. Then they learn to decide, for example, such factual matters as "who is doing what" in the story. They learn to perceive relationships among characters, to note the sequence of events, and sometimes to anticipate an outcome.

In interpreting a story that the teacher reads or tells, children respond to the words they hear, listening so that they can create in their own minds the pictures which are conjured up by the words the teacher speaks.

Both kinds of interpretation give the teacher an opportunity to begin the process of guiding boys' and girls' thinking by asking questions and by being careful to adjust the questions to the ability of the child addressed.

Chapter 4, as mentioned above, discusses listening skills in greater detail, and Chapters 5 and 6 explain in much more depth the nature of visual and interpretative skills at the pre-reading level. But these few suggestions may provide some idea of the kinds of activities that will be going on in the classroom during that important period when the teacher is introducing children to that most important concept—the relationship of spoken to printed language.

DEVELOPING AN UNDERSTANDING OF THE RELATION BETWEEN SPOKEN AND WRITTEN LANGUAGE

Before a child begins to associate printed words with meaning, he must understand how a printed word is related to a spoken word. He needs to realize that each printed word stands for just one spoken word and has the same meaning as that word. Gradually he will learn that while he sees a row of printed letters to make up a printed word, he hears a series of sounds that blend together to make up the corresponding spoken word. Other basic relationships between written and spoken language are sometimes referred to as "the conventions of written language." These include learning in a general way that print has a certain appearance on a page; that words are recorded with spaces between them; that sentences begin with big letters called capital letters; and that most sentences end with a dot called a period.

Children learn what sorts of things they may find expressed in print: facts (the way things are), experiences (things that happen), thoughts and feelings (things you think and feel but don't always say out loud), and dialogue (things you say).

They learn, also, that words go from left to right across the page and that for every spoken word there is always a corresponding written word. They begin to appreciate the difference between long and short words: Words that sound short when they are said usually look short when they are written, and words that take a longer time to say usually look longer when they are written.

Putting all of these discoveries together, children come ultimately to the one great realization that, as one little boy phrased it, "reading is just talk wrote down." With this realization, children are firmly on their way to successful experiences in learning how to read.

It isn't always as easy as adults may imagine for children to develop this understanding about the relationship between spoken and written language. It is especially difficult if the relationship is not properly explained and demonstrated before the child is expected to learn to read. One little boy who tried to read his pre-primers before he had grasped this fundamental information about printed words experienced a great disappointment. He waved his hand excitedly in class for permission to read a few lines of pre-primer text under an attractive picture. With considerable expression and animation, he gave a verbal interpretation of the picture, only to sit down in chagrin. That evening he told his parents sadly, "I read the *story* all right, but I said the wrong *words*."

That boy's disappointment came from his not understanding this important relationship between speech and print. He had recognized that the text under the picture had meaning and that the meaning was in the language, but he had not been shown that only one version of language could be acceptable for that page. He had found out the painful way that his own creative effort was not the same as "reading." Many of the youngsters who make up stories of their own while attempting to read lack a realization of this point-by-point correspondence between printed and spoken language.

Another worried beginner showed somewhat the same confusion when she asked her teacher doubtfully, "Does a printed word always say the same thing?" Adults should remember that we can call a picture of a cat either "pussy" or "kitten" or "cat" and that this freedom of nomenclature is something a small child brings to school with him. Therefore, it takes some new insights for him to realize that the printed word *cat* is "cat"—and that no variations will do.

Responding to words as symbols

In a way, a printed word is a symbol for a symbol and therefore derives its meaning in two steps. First, the printed word must be associated with the *sound* of the spoken word it represents. Second, it must be associated with the *meaning* of the spoken word. In the early stages of reading, a child may develop a habit of translating the printed text into a series of spoken words (or mental images of how the words would sound or feel, if spoken). Then, by understanding the meanings of the spoken words, he comprehends the meaning of the text.

In this manner, he may follow somewhat the same thinking pattern that a student of a foreign language follows when he translates the foreign words into English and then thinks the meanings in English. Both the beginning reader and the foreign-language student would do well to stress the meanings of words and try to think meanings from the beginning. The young reader should think what the printed symbols *mean*, along with what they say, and the foreign-language student should try to think meanings directly in the new language without the laborious process of translation. Early experiences in reading should be highly meaningful and purposive. As ability to read matures, the need to think of the spoken words decreases, until the absorbed reader is oblivious to all except meanings.

Introducing children to print

There are many ways in which children learn how spoken language is related to the conventions of our printed and written English. The first and most natural link between the child's world of speech and the adult world of print is, of course, the child's own name. No other spoken word has been heard over a longer period of time, and no other word has a meaning so close and personal to the child as the word that means himself. Because of its vivid meaning, it is probably an easier word to recall than any other word. It enters into almost every social experience the child has had, and, before he learned to use the substitute "I," he probably used the word to refer to himself. A card with his own name printed on it should be one of the child's earliest possessions at school.

For a time at the beginning of the school year, the child should be allowed to keep his own name card at his desk so that he can look at it often, touch it, examine it, become completely familiar with the way *his name* looks. Moving from this stage of familiarity with his name in print, the child may be encouraged to pick out his name from among a group of names placed on the chalk ledge or printed on the board. When a number of children in a group can successfully select their names from among others, they may be encouraged to try to copy their names either at the board or on large sheets of paper at their desks. If a group of names has been selected, several of which contain the same letters, children have an opportunity to notice the similarities in names and may be helped to form the individual letters. Thus, when Edward sees that his name begins with the same letter that Ethel's name begins with, he has already made the kind of observation about the printed symbols that is going to help him to recognize them, reproduce them, and read them.

At this stage of writing, children should be allowed to work freely, without guidelines, enjoying the pleasure of accomplishment and the pride of making their very own name, over and over again, in all sizes and styles.

Activities for relating spoken and written language

As children learn to identify and write their names they are learning something about the relation of a spoken word to a written word. This kind of learning is rapidly extended in other ways. For example, with some help from the teacher a class can formulate a record of one of their experiences. This class record, printed by the teacher at the children's dictation, will incorporate many of the conventions of our printed language.

A class that had a pet parakeet named Penny produced a story about one of their class adventures that centered around the bird. The pupils took daily turns feeding Penny, keeping careful track of whose turn it was by writing their own names on the board opposite the names of the days of the week, placed under the heading "Penny." One morning there was confusion. Somebody—nobody knew who—had erased some of the names, and the class wasn't sure who should feed Penny. Rudy, who thought it was his turn, went to the cage and opened it, but Theodore said it was his turn that day. Just then the fire alarm rang, and everybody walked out of the room very quickly. When they came back after the fire drill, the cage was empty. The story of how Penny was finally found was told by the youngsters themselves, edited by the teacher, and recorded by her on a large piece of drawing paper. The boys and girls signed their own names to the story, "Penny's Adventure," and mounted it on their bulletin board beside a picture of Penny that one of the boys drew. This is the story:

Penny's Adventure

Yesterday we had a fire drill.

We all had to go out.

The cage was open and Penny flew away.

We could not find her.

We looked and looked behind the screen.

Penny was not there.

All of a sudden we heard Penny chirp.

We turned as fast as our feet could move.

Guess where Penny was!

In another corner on a box stood Penny.

We put her in her cage.

And that was Penny's adventure.

In recording the story, the teacher used some simple devices to help the boys and girls see how each of the words she wrote down was related to what they were dictating to her. She said each word out loud when she wrote it down. When she started a sentence she said, "Now I am making a capital letter. You use a capital letter at the beginning of a sentence." The pupils watched while she made a capital letter. This procedure she followed for several sentences. Then when she started the next sentence, she asked, "How do I start this sentence?" This time the boys and girls could tell her that she should use a capital letter. Periods at the ends of sentences were explained in a similar manner. At first the teacher said, "Now I am making a period. When I come to the end of the sentence, I make a period. The period shows where the sentence ends." Occasionally she omitted a period to see if anyone noticed. Whoever noticed that she had left out a period was permitted to come up to the board and put it in.

Learning how sentences look.   Gradually the boys and girls in this class grew accustomed to seeing how sentences look when they are written down—a capital letter at the beginning, a period at the end, or sometimes an exclamation point. They saw that words always go from left to right in a straight line and that between each word there is always a space. In the story "Penny's Adventure" they could see the difference between long words and short words. Words like *yesterday* and *adventure* that took quite a long time to say also took a long time to write and looked like long words in the story. Words that were quick to say, like *we* and *go*, were words that were quick to write and looked short on the board. Out of all this, the pupils made the generalization that there was a relation between the sound of a word and the way that word looked when it was written.

Making up a story about a class experience led some of the boys and girls to want to tell stories about what had happened to them outside of school. The teacher encouraged these pupils to tell their stories and then helped them by editing and recording their stories in the same way she had recorded "Penny's Adventure." All the boys and girls in the class helped the teacher do the recording by watching carefully to be sure she wrote the sentences correctly with

capital letters, spaces between words, and periods. Thus, everybody had still further experience with the way the English language is written. Two of the pupils drew illustrations for their stories, and these pictures, along with the story texts as recorded by the teacher and signed by the pupils, were put up on the bulletin board with the story of Penny's adventure.

One of the stories was about a day when it was cold outside and there was ice all over the playground.

Ice! Ice! Ice!

We were playing on the ice.

I was the policeman.

I said, "Stop! Nobody can go by!"

But they couldn't stop.

They just slid and slid.

And then they fell down.

When the teacher came to the third line of this story, she said, "Now we have to make some new punctuation, because this line of Paul's story tells what somebody said. When you tell what somebody said, you have to put quotation marks around it—like this." And she put the quotation marks in as she said this.

The next story was about a rainy day:

Walking in the Rain

I had an old brown umbrella.

My sister Kate had a new yellow umbrella.

But my little sister Jean didn't have any.

Then grandma gave her a blue umbrella.

We all went walking in the rain.

We had lots of fun.

We got all wet.

After this, many more stories were told and recorded, while the boys and girls watched to see that each time somebody dictated a word, a word was written to go with it, and that each sentence began with a capital letter and ended with a period.

Learning what sentences can say.   After several experiences with telling and recording stories, the teacher asked the class what kinds of things they believed could be told in writing. They all thought very carefully about the stories they had dictated and recorded. They decided that writing could tell what happened, what people said, what people thought but didn't say, what color things were or how big they were or something else about how they looked. And it could show when somebody was surprised or excited if you used an exclamation point instead of a period at the end of an idea.

FROM UNDERSTANDING TO SKILL

The children in the class described above had absorbed thoroughly the idea that print is talk written down. They had learned what to expect when they began to read. They knew how words would look. They knew they would have to begin at the left side of the line of words and go across to the right. They knew how the beginning of a sentence would look and how they would know where the end was. They had, in fact, a solid introduction to some of the most important conventions of written and printed English and, along with that, a working understanding of the relation between spoken and written language.

BIBLIOGRAPHY

Durkin, Dolores. "Reading Instruction and the Five-Year-Old Child," *Challenge and Experiment in Reading* (International Reading Association Conference Proceedings, Vol. 7, 1962), 23-27. Provides help for the kindergarten teacher in planning a program adapted to the individual differences within her class. Includes concrete suggestions for an "exposure curriculum" at the kindergarten level.

Hughes, Marie M., and Sanchez, George I. *Learning a New Language.* General Service Bulletin No. 101. Washington: Association for Childhood Education International, 1958. Describes the growth of language in relation to the child's environment. Gives special attention to the limitations imposed on the child who enters school with a language handicap.

Mackintosh, Helen K. "How Fundamental Are the Language Arts?" *Childhood Education,* 35 (December 1958), 157-161. Points out the importance of skill in language as a basis for all subsequent learning. Gives special attention to the individual teacher's role in helping children develop language skills.

Morrison, Ida E., and Perry, I. F. *Kindergarten-Primary Education—Teaching Procedures.* New York: Ronald Press Co., 1961. Stresses fundamental principles of growth and learning. Part II deals with reading; Part III, with development of oral language.

Russell, David H. *Children's Thinking.* Boston: Ginn and Company, 1956. Brings together findings from studies in child psychology and educational psychology and relates them to problems of improving thinking ability in the classroom.

chapter four

Pupils Use Their Ears

A mother once called her actively playing two-year-old to come in for his nap. "Don't say that, Mommy," he protested. Then, putting his hands over his ears, he looked up impishly and said, "Now you *can't* talk!"

Speech is certainly closely related to hearing. When no one is listening, speech serves little purpose, and the job of learning to speak a language presents almost insuperable obstacles to one who has never had an opportunity to hear the sounds and cadences of the language.

Hearing is first of all a physiological process, depending on the functioning of the ears, brain, and coordinating nerve pathways. But hearing is much more than physiological capability. Hearing is also a consciously directed response to sound, the making of careful distinctions among sounds, and the associating of meaning with sound. This consciously directed response to the auditory stimulus is usually called not just "hearing" but "listening."

One of the big jobs of the teacher during the pre-reading period is helping children to develop some skill in this very necessary business of listening. As was suggested in Chapter 3, the development of listening skills is basic to the development of oral language, which in turn provides a foundation for interpreting written language.

PRESCHOOL LISTENING EXPERIENCES

Sound constitutes a normal part of our lives, and it might be supposed that the child who comes to school has "just naturally" learned how to listen. All the evidence that we have suggests that this is not necessarily the case. The child has heard a great deal—pleasant sounds and unpleasant sounds—but he may have listened very little. That is, he may not have given very much conscious, discriminating attention to the particular characteristics of the sounds which have been a part of his environment.

The sounds he may have heard cover a wide range. With rare and unusual exceptions, children have heard language. They have learned to associate meaning with the sounds of language, and they have heard these sounds accurately enough to be able to reproduce them, or an approximation of them. They have heard also a great many sounds other than human speech. Children in rural areas—now a small percentage of the children in the United States—have heard a variety of sounds in the world of nature and also, in most cases, the sound of machinery, trucks, and automobiles. Children in small and middle-sized urban communities have had a somewhat similar blend of the natural and the mechanical, with probably more noise from automotive traffic and fewer of the sounds of the open country. In large urban areas most children have heard none of the sounds of the country, but are more likely to be surrounded by mechanical noises: the roar of automobiles on a throughway, the shrieking of the elevated, the clatter of the subway, the grinding of gears, and the hiss of air brakes.

The sounds of television and radio are familiar to almost all children—country, city, or town. Many have heard phonograph records—even the new stereo recordings. A few fortunate children may have enjoyed some live music, perhaps at an outdoor concert or at home, if adults in the family play musical instruments. Some may have attended nursery schools, where they heard stories and poems read aloud and perhaps played in rhythm bands. Some may have had stories read to them at home. Some may know the roar and whistle of jets overhead; others may know factory whistles, jack hammers, or pneumatic drills.

These and many other sounds have been a part of the lives of children before they come to school. These are the sounds they have *heard* but not necessarily *listened* to. In fact, with all their variety of experience with sounds, children seem to have one characteristic in common when they start school: they have not necessarily learned how to listen.

LEARNING HOW TO LISTEN

One of the causes of not listening is symbolized by the boy described in the opening paragraph of this chapter—the one who covered his ears to keep out his mother's unwelcome words. Too many of the scraps of language thrown at a small child are commands (to do something he doesn't want to do), prohibitions (against doing something he wants to do), exclamations of shock, anger, displeasure, disgust. The child is all too familiar with: "MauREEN! . . . You spilled your OATmeal! . . . Get back in bed THIS MINUTE! . . . STOP that! . . . MauREEN! . . . You're all DIRTY! . . ." Little wonder that many children develop invisible "earlids" that they turn down conveniently to block out the shrill, unwanted voice of authority that seems forever to signify something unpleasant.

Not wanting to hear, then, is one cause for not listening; another is *not needing to hear*. Commands not obeyed the first time are sure to be repeated, probably several times—and, just as predictably, each time in a louder voice than before. Any observant child readily discovers that careful attention to the first performance is therefore clearly a great waste of time and energy!

Still another cause of not listening may be the sheer quantity of noise assaulting a child's eardrums, much of it unpleasant. The dripping faucet in the kitchen sink, the high-pitched whine of the vacuum cleaner, the monotonous "whursh-whursh" of cars going by on an expressway—the capacity to block these noises out of one's consciousness can be as vital to mental health and mental growth as the capacity to tune in on sounds which should be attended to.

One of the big jobs of the classroom teacher is to help the child discover which sounds are to be listened to and which are to be ignored. This is not as easy as it may sound. Many an adult, having accustomed himself to not listening to a commercial on radio or television, discovers just too late that he has forgotten to "tune back in" in time to pick up the weather or the news report he wanted to hear. The child is confronted with the same dilemma.

In the classroom, for example, the pupil has to learn which sounds are to be listened to and which are to be ignored. External sounds are usually to be ignored—sounds such as sirens, buses, playground shouts, ice-cream vendors' bells, and noise from other classes or from other groups in the same classroom. If a child is discovered listening to such sounds he is admonished to "pay attention," which translated means "stop listening to that sound." On the other hand, he is expected to listen to the sounds made by his own group in the classroom. If he ignores these sounds, he receives the same type of admonition he received for listening to the other sounds.

Eyes are conveniently provided with eyelids which may be closed to shut out what the viewer does not wish to see. Similarly, eyes may be opened at will so as to see what one wants to see. Ears are not so conveniently equipped— there aren't any "earlids" to open and close at will. Only persons who wear a hearing aid have a handy means of tuning out sounds they don't want to hear, like screeching tires or dull conversations. Children must get along without such a convenient device. Simply by an act of will they must learn to listen or not to listen to the sounds around them. Often, in fact, they must simultaneously *not listen* to one group of sounds and *listen* to other sounds. Or they must remember, after they have carefully "tuned out" one set of sounds, to "tune in" again at the right time so that they won't miss what they are supposed to hear.

SUGGESTIONS FOR DEVELOPING LISTENING SKILLS

It is a wise teacher who can successfully teach children to be sensitive to some sounds and, at the same time, to be insensitive to others. And yet most of living requires that people make such distinctions. If possible, the teacher needs to create a new atmosphere for listening—an atmosphere in which children want to attend to certain sounds, because it is fun to do so, and in which they want to develop sensitivity to certain sounds, because the ability to discriminate correctly leads to pleasant rewards.

Characteristics of sounds

A good place to begin in developing this kind of sensitivity is with a study of certain characteristics of sounds. Sounds differ from one another in many ways. Some are louder, softer, higher, lower, shorter, longer, purer, or more complex than others. Calling attention to the various characteristics of sounds will help the children to become aware of these characteristics and to distinguish among certain characteristics which were previously undifferentiated. The following section presents some of the ways in which a teacher may sensitize children to the intensity, pitch, quality, and duration and sequence of sounds.

Intensity. One of the characteristics of every sound is its intensity. Sounds may be so soft that they are almost inaudible or so loud that they are painful. It is difficult to listen for long to sounds one can barely hear. It is also hard to attend to overly loud voices. One quickly turns down the volume of a radio or television set when the sounds suddenly blare out too loud for comfort. We listen best to voices that are gauged to a comfortable volume— that can be heard easily but are not too loud.

Spoken language varies constantly in intensity. Within a word the accented syllable is louder than the unaccented, as in *bas*ket and po*ta*to. Within a sentence certain words are stressed for emphasis, such as "I've looked *everywhere*." Within a longer thought unit, the stress is on the more important sentences or varies in response to the feelings and emotions of the speaker. Listening attentively for changes in the loudness or softness of sounds helps children become aware of this quality in language.

Games that call attention to intensity. A game that calls attention to the intensity, or loudness and softness, of sounds is the simple act of marching to music, stamping loudly when the music is loud, tiptoeing quietly when the music is soft. Children enjoy the physical activity of this game, which can be played first with the whole group and later with individuals who need additional help. The teacher may stop the music suddenly and ask, "Was the music *loud* or *soft* when I stopped it?" A middle degree of loudness may be introduced as children gain proficiency by having them stamp for the loudest, walk for the medium loud, and tiptoe for the softest music.

Another game that requires reacting to sound intensities is "Hide the Thimble." Place a thimble (or any small classroom object) in full view but in an unexpected place while one child is out of the room. When he returns, direct his hunting by clapping loudly when he approaches the thimble and softly when he goes away from it. Draw from the children a verbal explanation of the game, using the words *louder* and *softer*.

Compare the sounds made by ringing a large bell and a small bell; or by blowing a big toy horn and a little one; or by dropping an eraser and a block of wood. Other comparisons of loud and soft might be made by tapping on a desk and on a folded piece of cloth; by comparing the sounds of a ticking alarm clock and a wrist watch; by walking and then tiptoeing across the room; by slamming a door and then closing it gently. In each case, ask which of each pair of sounds is the *louder* one, which the *softer* one.

Voices, too, may be used to compare the intensity of sounds. Playing train is a good game to call attention to the fact that voices can produce louder or softer sounds. Place a chair at the center front of the classroom for use as the station. Choose a child to sit in the station, waiting for the train. Begin with a train of three children who stand in the back of the room and chant, "clickety-click, clickety-click, clickety-click," "dig-a-dig, dig-a-dig, dig-a-dig," or any other appropriate train sound that can be vocalized. Each child places his hands on the shoulders of the child in front. Then, chanting softly, the train marches in line toward the front of the room, increasing the volume of the chant until it arrives at the station. Then the train stops, the passenger gets on by placing his hands on the shoulders of the last child, and the train goes on its way to the back of the room, the voices becoming softer and softer as the train goes "far away." While the train is in the back of the room, the teacher (or a child) quietly taps another passenger, who takes a seat in the station and joins the train when it returns, as before, until all children are on the train. Have the children explain when their voices are to be *soft* and when *loud* in this game.

If an airplane passes over the school, stop for a moment and listen. Have the children notice how loud the noise is as the airplane flies over; how soft the sound is as the airplane recedes into the distance. Imitate the sound vocally, letting the voice become softer and softer.

After the story or poetry hour, make use of opportunities to note the stress on certain words. Many stories and rhymes contain a word or phrase or sentence which is given unusual stress. A teacher who is alert to possibilities for auditory training may, at the conclusion of the story, help the children to identify the loud or soft parts. "When the little engine said, 'I *think* I can,' which part did he say *loudest*?" "Which part did the little gingerbread boy say *loudest* when he said, 'And I can run away from *you*, I can, I can'?" This training should not interrupt the fun and excitement of the story in any way; it should consist of just a casual remark or question before the children go on to another story or activity.

Pitch. Sounds are high or low. Mice and birds produce sounds of high vibration frequency. A bass viol or bass drum produces sounds of low vibration frequency. Sounds of human speech vary in pitch. Most men have voices of much lower pitch than women, and children's voices are usually higher than those of adults. Each speaker varies the pitch of his voice so as to convey his meaning. A rising pitch of the voice at the end of a sentence may indicate that the sentence is a question. Within a longer thought unit, whole sentences are raised or lowered in pitch for various dramatic purposes. For example, notice the pitch changes in a speaker's voice during the relating of "The Three Bears." Children love to listen for and to imitate the low tones of Father Bear's voice as contrasted with the high, squeaky voice of Baby Bear. Emotions, too, are communicated by changes of pitch—by the shrill, high sounds of alarm, for example, and the low tones of reassurance.

A flexible voice that readily lifts or lowers in pitch attracts and holds attention. In fact, it is difficult to attend long to a monotone or even to understand all that is being said, so much do pitch changes contribute not only to listening comfort but to the actual meaning of language.

Games that call attention to pitch. The children's attention may be directed to the pitch of sounds by having them listen to a note struck on the piano, then to a note struck an octave above the first. Repeat such sequences several times. While the high note is being struck, ask the children to stand tall with arms high above head; while the low note is being struck, ask them to squat low. Do this for several different octaves, using the terms *high* and *low* to describe the relative position of the two sounds. Allow children to take turns at the piano to strike high or low notes of their own selection. It is not necessary for them to find the octave; they can strike any high key and any low one and experiment with the tones. This game can be used as a "quickie" for a moment's rest from seat activities, because of the lively exercise in alternate standing and squatting.

The previous game may be extended by playing up and down the scale. First, strike one note on a piano or toy xylophone, letting the children listen closely; then strike the next note above or below or the same one again. Children respond "higher," "lower," or "same." Play up the scale, letting the children respond "higher, higher, higher." Play down the scale as the children say "lower, lower, lower" to each succeeding note. Then make three or four stairsteps—say from floor to small chair, from small chair to the teacher's chair, and then to a table. Let the children take turns in going up and down the steps while notes are being struck in the sequence of the partial scale. Then strike the notes in mixed order and see whether the children can find the proper steps.

Differences in pitch may also be observed during the story hour. "The Three Bears" is a favorite story whose charm, as mentioned before, is largely due to the pitch differences in the voices of the characters. Stories of elves and fairies, or tales in which mice or crickets are personified, give the children a chance to use and hear high-pitched voices. On the other hand, the voices of talking elephants, giants, trolls, and other large creatures should be appropriately dramatized in low tones. Using the terms *high* and *low* in referring to these voices helps to direct children's listening to this characteristic of the sounds they hear.

Quality. Each musical instrument has a characteristic quality. Quality may be defined as the characteristic of a tone that distinguishes it from other tones of the same pitch and loudness. For example, the note A above middle C on an oboe may be easily distinguished from the same A on a clarinet or on a French horn. That certain something that distinguishes it is its quality.

The simplest and most uninteresting musical tone is the tone of a tuning fork. This tone, with its characteristic "pure" or "empty" quality, is produced by vibrations of one frequency only—that is, the fork vibrates only at its fundamental or named frequency. The A tuning fork vibrates purely at 440 vibrations per second, the frequency of A above middle C. This is the pure or fundamental tone. Musical instruments producing this same pitch do not produce "pure" tones. Instead, their tones are enriched by a variety of overtones, or upper partials, which are present in varying strengths, producing by their unique combinations the characteristic quality of the instrument. Most musical tones include, for example, the pitch one octave above the fundamental. The teacher may discover this for herself by depressing—without striking—one key in the middle range of the piano and holding it down, while striking forcibly and releasing the key one octave lower. The open string of the depressed key will then be heard to respond (vibrate) in sympathy with the vibrations of the first overtone of the struck key; that is, the sound that persists will be a pitch one octave above the key struck, a pitch that was not *struck* at all.

A trained ear can hear the two frequencies vibrating simultaneously in the sound of the lower note. The pitch an octave above is, of course, not the only overtone present in a musical tone, although it is frequently the strongest. The unique combination of remaining overtones creates the individual quality that is identified with a particular instrument such as the oboe, flute, or bassoon.

The human voice, similarly, is a unique combination of fundamental pitch and overtones. The singing voice is composed of partials of regular frequency and thus produces tones as does any other musical instrument. The speaking voice also includes various noises—that is, sounds of irregular frequency—and consequently a different range of qualities. The speaking voice is described, for example, as nasal, denasal, harsh, mellow, shrill, or whining. In the case of the human voice, the individual quality results from the individual manner of producing tone through a characteristic use of mouth, teeth, nose, vocal cords, and breathing apparatus. The change of voice quality when one has a head cold is a common phenomenon. The nasal resonating chambers are closed off, which changes the balance of overtones present. The familiar result is the denasal quality of "I have a cold id by dose."

Games that call attention to quality. The game "Who said it?" is fun for all and emphasizes the discrimination of voice quality. Four or five children are chosen to stand in a row before the rest of the class, whose eyes are covered and who are instructed not to peek. The teacher touches one of the children, who says "Good morning" or something else appropriate. The class uncover their eyes and someone guesses who spoke. After each child in the front row has said "Good morning" in his natural voice and has been correctly guessed, the teacher again touches a child. This time, he attempts to disguise his voice. When identified, he must sit down, and the game continues—usually amidst much giggling, for there is always something very funny to six-year-olds about a disguised voice, probably because they can still hear the original quality and catch the culprit. The teacher may add to the fun by unexpectedly saying "Good morning" herself in place of one of the front-row children.

Other games requiring sensitivity to quality may be played with a variety of props. One child may stand behind a screen at the front of the room creating various sound effects. The other children guess what is being done to produce the sound. Sound effects which may be used include: shaking a rattle, turning an eggbeater, sharpening a pencil, crushing a piece of paper, pouring water from a bottle into a glass, popping a balloon, blowing a whistle, tooting a horn, sawing a piece of wood, hammering a nail, or ringing a bell. The teacher may call attention to the characteristic quality of the sound by using descriptive words such as *whir, swish, rattle, crash, bang, clack, buzz, click, squeak, murmur, rumble, snort, hiss,* and *gurgle.*

Children also enjoy trying to imitate certain sounds. They may make the sound of rain by drumming with their fingers; of wind, by blowing through a tube; of a galloping horse, by tapping with sticks on a box; of ocean waves, by letting sand roll back and forth in a box; or of fire, by crumpling cellophane.

Duration and sequence.　　Sounds last for shorter or longer periods of time and follow one another in sequence. Sometimes language sounds are produced, one after another, in a fast staccato rhythm, at other times in slow legato. Talking takes time. Even the most rapid speaker cannot say everything at once—he must follow a sequence in articulating one sound after another to form a word, one word after another to form a sentence, and one sentence after another to form a longer unit of language.

Games that call attention to duration and sequence. Children's attention may be called to the duration and sequence of sounds by producing prolonged or short tones on a musical instrument and using the terms *long* and *short* to describe the length of duration of each tone. Use the terms *first sound* and *last sound* in this game—"The *first* sound was longer than the *last* sound."

It is difficult for anyone to estimate or compare two time units without some measure or time beat; hence rhythmical games of all kinds are helpful activities for developing awareness of the shorter time units within a longer duration. Skipping, galloping, marching, and dancing to music all emphasize "keeping time." Fast rhythms and slow rhythms can be contrasted by letting the children run fast or walk slowly according to the tempo of the music. A rhythm band of toy instruments—bells, horns, triangles, and quickly improvised drums such as a chalk box and sticks—can be assembled to the delight of all. Let children take turns being the leader. The leader sets the rhythm by waving his baton, and all play joyously, trying to keep time with the beat given. After the children have mastered the simple *dot-dot-dot-dot* rhythm at different speeds, they may try the *dot-dit-dit, dot-dit-dit* of the waltz rhythm.

Tap on the desk in an irregular sequence of three to five taps, and have the children try to imitate the series—for example, *tap-tap-*(rest)*-tap, tap-tap-tap-*(rest)*-tap-tap; tap-*(rest)*-tap-tap.* Play the game of "Echo" by letting one child tap four or five times and then having another child across the room echo back more softly the same sequence of taps.

Produce three sounds (ring a bell, tap on the table, shake a rattle) and let a child imitate the sequence. Have other children tell which sound was *first,* which was *last,* and which was in the *middle.* Produce three tones of different durations. Have the children tell the position of the *longest* tone and of the *shortest* tone. For example, "The *longest* tone was the *middle* one."

Sensitivity to the duration and sequence of language can be developed through jingles and rhymes. "Hippety-hop to the barber shop" gives an energizing rhythm that encourages skipping to the beat or accent. If a child says "hippety hoppety to the barber shop," he is likely to be thrown off beat and lose step. He must give the exact words in their proper sequence and accent if he is to come out even with the saying and the skipping.

The teacher may ask, "What did we say just after *hippety?*—after *barber?*" To answer correctly, the children must have a clear recognition of the sequence of the language sounds in the jingle. The teacher may also ask, "Which takes the longer to say, *hippety* or *hop?*" To answer this question the children must be able to detect the difference in duration of the two words.

Developing sensitivity to sounds in words

Children who have learned to recognize the differences between sounds that are soft and loud, high and low, long and short, first and last; who can describe a few sounds in verbal terms such as *like a bell, a crash, a bang, a whisper,* or *a buzz,* and so on; and who have developed sensitivity to rhythm and time beat are ready for the next steps in the auditory program—that of making the finer judgments and discriminations necessary to hear, within the total auditory impression of a word, the initial and final sounds and to detect slight sound differences between words.

When children first begin to learn to read, they associate the total visual impression of the printed pattern with the total auditory impression of the language pattern and its attendant meanings. Not until the child has a need to attack new words by noting their phonetic or structural details is his attention called to the relationships between the visual patterns and the sound patterns (such as noting that *boy* and *ball* both look and sound alike at the beginning).

Differences in sounds. If children have not learned to think about the sounds of words and have not differentiated their various qualities, they may be at a loss to understand how sounds could give a cue to an unknown printed word. At the same time, they are encountering so many new words in reading that it becomes an increasingly difficult task to remember them all by sight, and some method of attack is imperative. Children who have had delightful times with the early pre-primer stories may discover that now "Reading's getting hard." Often teachers try belatedly to hurry the children by using phonetic drills that require ability to make auditory discriminations and associations at a higher level than the children are prepared for. Many reading difficulties begin at this time, as children become discouraged and resistant. Parents seek out reading clinics with the complaint that "My child can't sound his words."

The situation described above need not exist if children are given opportunity to develop the auditory skills slowly, step by step, throughout the entire reading-readiness programs of kindergarten and first grade. Long before the child is expected to use auditory skills in reading, his concepts of sounds have been growing and maturing. Comparing the sounds of words has become such a part of his thinking that he can readily call to mind many words that begin with the same sound (such as *ball, boy, box, bunny*) or that rhyme (such as *ran, can, man, fan*). He has such a rich background of experiences with sounds that when the teacher explains how the sounds of words are related to the printed text in reading, he is able to understand the relationship. Thereafter, he finds it easy and natural to use his knowledge of sounds in attacking new printed words, and he progresses rapidly in reading as he develops increasing independence.

The game "Which is it?" is fun for little children, for it smacks of a riddle. Select a number of word pairs on the basis of some gross similarity in sound of the total word, such as *feathers, sweaters; desk, nest; chickens, children; puddle, puppy; Indian, engine.* Ask, "Which grow on chickens—feathers or sweaters?" "Where do birds lay their eggs—in a desk or in a nest?" "Which have wings—children or chickens?" "Which is an animal—a puppy or a puddle?" "Which lives in a wigwam—an Indian or an engine?"

Continue with questions answerable by one member of each word pair. If the children do well with these, ask, "Can we ride on a penny?" Suggest that we ride on a pony, not on a penny. "Can we climb a letter?" (No, a ladder.) Or, for variation, ask, "Is a chair a jar?" "Is a monkey some money?" "Is a bottle a bubble?" "Is an elephant an envelope?" Obtain simple definitions to be sure the children recognize the differences in meaning between each pair of similar-sounding words.

A page for testing and training can be arranged as follows. Each box contains two pictures of objects whose names are grossly similar in sound, such as *turkey, turtle; horse, house; whistle, window; table, cradle; eggs, ax; drum, broom.*

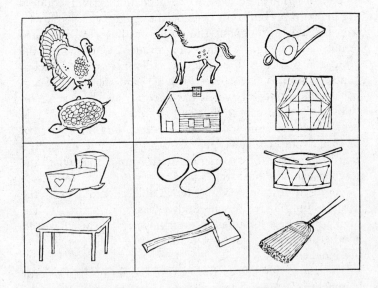

First, name the objects in each box so that the children will know which words the pictures illustrate and will not identify the cradle as a bed, the ax as a hammer, or the horse as a pony. Then say, "In the top row [indicate by sweeping hand] mark the turtle, mark the horse, mark the window. Now in the bottom row [indicating] mark the cradle, mark the ax, mark the drum." A child who has difficulty in discriminating gross sound differences may be discovered, since he may hear *ax* as *eggs*, and thus mark the eggs, or show some other revealing confusion. This page and others like it may be used for practice in naming objects until the child can pronounce each pair of words distinctly and can point to the correct one of any pair from hearing the word pronounced.

Rhyming words. Throughout the child's preschool and kindergarten experiences with nursery rhymes and jingles, he has been developing sensitivity to rhyming words even though he probably has not identified them as rhymes. As soon as he is familiar with a number of jingles, give him opportunity to complete a jingle by supplying the last or rhyming word. Children are often able to do this long before they can repeat the entire jingle from memory or have any concept of what a rhyme is: "Jack and Jill went up the _____," "Seesaw Marjory _____," "Jack be nimble, Jack be quick, Jack jump over the candle_____." Jingles ring so in our ears that the rhyming words pop into our minds almost without bidding.

Call the children's attention to the fact that the rhyming words sound alike. "Jack and *Jill* went up the *hill—Jill* sounds like _____?" Do this for many rhymes until the children not only hear that the two accented words sound alike but can also think back into the rhyme and find the word that sounds like the final word. "Jack be nimble, Jack be quick, Jack jump over the candlestick—*stick* sounds like _____?" It requires thinking power and real ability to make the auditory judgment when the child is asked to select the rhyming word from the words previously said.

After the children have mastered this level of detecting rhymes, see if they can think of words, not in the jingle, that sound like *Jill* and *hill*. At first the teacher may give a list. "*Jill* isn't the only word that sounds like *hill*. I am going to tell you some other words that sound like *hill—mill, pill, fill*." Do the same with the rhyming words from many jingles until the children can give a list of three or four rhyming words whenever the teacher gives a jingle and starts a list. At first the children will merely repeat words they have heard in the teacher's list, but soon other rhyming words will be suggested. About this time, begin to use the term *rhyme*—"*Saw* rhymes with *Daw* and also rhymes with *paw, raw, caw, straw.*" "*Quick* rhymes with *stick.* All these words rhyme—*quick, stick, Dick, pick, tick.*"

A page of pictures containing pairs of words that rhyme may be made for further diagnosis and practice. Select also, as foils, several pairs of words that do *not* rhyme. Before beginning the exercise, name each picture so that the children will know which words are illustrated and will not call the *coat* a *jacket*, or the *man, Father*.

Indicating the page, say, "There are two pictures in each box. In some boxes the names of the pictures rhyme. In other boxes the names of the pictures do not rhyme. If the names rhyme, you may mark the pictures. If the names do not rhyme, do not mark the pictures. We will do the first two together. *Goat, coat*—do they rhyme?" Suggest that they do. "Mark the goat and the coat. That's fine. Look at the next box. *Orange, apple*—do they rhyme?" Draw out agreement that they do not. Say, "Then we won't mark the orange and the apple. Now say the names of the other pictures to yourself and mark the ones that rhyme."

The page of pictures has diagnostic value in showing which children are able to hear the rhymes. Those who do not succeed with the page need more experience with rhymes and jingles. They may practice saying and listening to pairs of words that do or do not rhyme until they are able to do this and similar pages accurately.

Teachers who are clever at drawing pictures on the blackboard may make up the first part of a jingle and draw three pictures from which children may select the completing rhyme. These should be drawn previous to the game and named, so that the children will not call the *shoe* a *slipper* or a *pump*. Examples follow.

Teacher: I bought something new.

It is a pretty _____.

Pointing to the three pictures, she asks, "Which did I buy? Something that rhymes with *new*." The children name the correct picture and then give the entire jingle.

Teacher: Go look in the hall

And find your _____.

The children name the correct picture and again give the entire jingle.

Let the children try to make their own jingles. These (as well as the teacher's) may be the sheerest doggerel, with missing beats in the meter, but if the rhyme is there, give delighted approval.

After the children can use the term *rhyme*, can tell whether or not two words rhyme, can supply missing rhymes, and can perhaps even compose little rhymes of their own, see if they can make still finer auditory discriminations. Select a picture such as the following, with one object followed by two other objects. The name of one of the latter two objects rhymes with the first one; the other does not rhyme but is selected as a foil on the basis of some other similarity in sound to the first word. The

teacher pronounces the names of all three objects. The children mark the one of the pair whose name rhymes with that of the first object. To succeed with a page of this kind, the children must be able to recognize the exact way in which rhyming words sound alike. Just any similarity in sound, such as *horse, house,* doesn't make a rhyme. The teacher says: "*Gate—goat, skate;* mark the one that rhymes with *gate.* Next row: *house—mouse, horse;* mark the one that rhymes with *house.*"

The previous exercise may be stepped up to a still higher level of difficulty by placing the three pictures in a row, having the pictures named, and then asking the children to mark the two whose names rhyme. The children now have no pattern to match but must find the rhymes for themselves. Always remember to pronounce the words first so the children will know what words the pictures stand for. It would spoil the purpose of the page if a child called a *dish* a *plate*, for example. In the rows of pictures below, the words are *fish, fork, dish,* and *boat, coat, bat.*

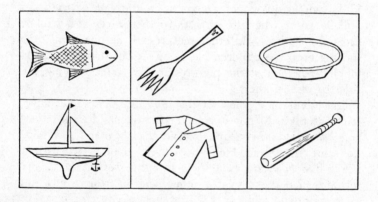

Alliteration. At the same time that children are becoming familiar with rhymes, they should also have many opportunities for noticing alliteration, or words that begin with the same sound. The tuneful alliterative phrases in jingles and stories are constantly catching attention and should be repeated for sheer pleasure. Billy *goats gruff* that go *trip trap* on the *troll's* bridge are fun to hear and tell about, because of the alliteration. The alliterative *hippety-hop* of the barber shop jingle is just as ear-tickling as the rhyme of *hop* and *shop. Pease porridge; dickory, dock; Baa, baa, black* . . . ; *a diller, a dollar; a-sailing on the sea; Jack and Jill; Little Lucy Locket,* and many other combinations of words beginning alike add their share to the delightful qualities of nursery rhymes. At first, merely give the children the experiences of hearing and enjoying the sounds.

Cut out pictures from magazines that illustrate alliteration, such as a picture of a pig in a pen, a baby in a bed or in a bathtub, a horse eating hay, a house on a hill, a boy with a ball or a bicycle, a girl with a goat. Mount the pictures on cards of the same size or on 9″ x 12″ tagboard. Show about five cards at first, simply telling the children that the pictures are about things that are fun to hear and say. While showing each picture, pronounce the "title" with emphasis on the alliteration. Then ask for a volunteer to repeat what was said for each picture. By the time several children have repeated "A Pig in a Pen," "A House on a Hill," while looking at the pictures, the rest of the class will be saying the catchy titles to themselves and will be eager for a turn. Add other pictures to the pile from time to time until the children have quite a tall stack. Let pairs of children look at the pictures at their tables, saying the titles to one another.

Call attention to the fact that *boy* and *ball* sound alike, but that they do not rhyme. Have the children say *boy* and *ball* very slowly, and explain that *boy* and *ball* have the same first sound. Help them think of other words that begin like *boy* and *ball*, such as *baby, basket, boat*, and *birthday*. Do the same for other pairs of words, *girl* and *goat*, supplying additional words such as *go, garden, guess*, and *gate*.

If a child has difficulty in understanding that words have a beginning sound, explain further in some such way as this: "Can you say *Mother?* Now, say *Mother* very slowly like this [drawling out the word, but not separating the sounds]. You see, we don't say *Mother* all at once. We begin to say it and then we say the rest of the word. Put your lips together and just *begin* to say *Mother*. Now just *begin* to say *man*. Your lips feel just like they did when you got ready to say *Mother*, don't they? *Mother* and *man* begin with the same sound. *Mother, man, moon, monkey, milk*, all sound alike at the beginning. They feel alike on our lips, too."

Pictures may be arranged showing pairs of objects whose names do or do not begin with the same sound. Name the pairs of objects and have the children mark only those whose names begin with the same sound. In the illustration following, the pairs of words are: Top row—*boy, ball; train, blocks; fish, fan.* Bottom row—*saw, soap; leaf, lamp; shoe, boy.* A page of this kind has diagnostic value for finding the children who are ready to make such fine discriminations successfully. Those who are not ready should

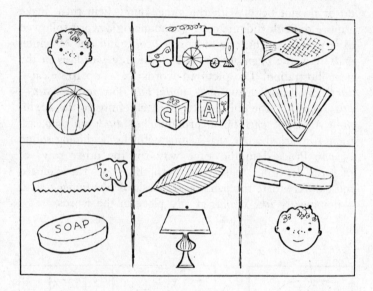

be given extra practice with auditory games (such as "A Pig in the Pen" cards) or with additional pages of pictures arranged like the last illustration.

Another game which can be played at the table is to give the children brightly colored magazine pictures containing many objects. Draw a ring around one of the objects in each picture. Let the children study the picture to find the names of other objects that begin with the same sound as the name of the encircled object. The children place a marker (button, dried pumpkin seed, grain of corn, small disk, or any similar object) on each object they find. For example, if the picture shows a child's nursery room with toys and the teacher has encircled the *ball*, markers might be placed on the *bed, baby, books, boat,* or whatever else can be found in the pictures that begins like *ball*. By encircling an object beginning with a different sound for each picture (making sure there are several objects that can be found easily), the teacher may redistribute the pictures until each child has worked with each picture.

After the children are able to tell whether two words do or do not begin with the same sound, help them make a more difficult judgment by pronouncing a word followed by a pair of words, one of which *begins* and one of which *ends* with the *beginning* sound of the key word, as in the next illustration. The pictured words are: Top row: *cat— duck, can*. Middle row: *ball—book, bib*. Bottom row: *sun— bus, soap*. Ask the children to listen carefully to the *beginning* sound of *cat*. Then, pronouncing *duck* and *can*, ask them to mark the one that begins with the beginning sound of *cat*. Proceed in the same way for the other rows of pictures. In order to succeed with this page, the children must differentiate the pairs on the basis of *like initial sounds* —not merely *like sounds* at any place in the words.

Next, set up a page of pictures in which the children are given three words and are asked to decide which two begin with the same sound. The children now have no word pattern to give a cue to the sound. In the illustration that follows, the pictured words are: Top row: *top, table, hat*. Middle row: *pig, cup, pie*. Bottom row: *bib, bottle, bat*.

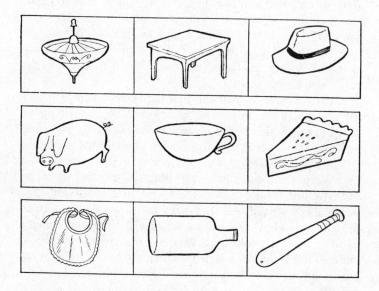

Pronounce the three words pictured. Then say "Mark the two that *begin* with the same sound."

Isolated speech sounds. Sometimes an isolated speech sound has a meaning of its own in language. For example, in playing house or singing the baby to sleep, the children may say "sh," holding fingers to lips. Other speech sounds are associated with activities or with objects. Children may give the sound "wh" in blowing out the candles of a birthday cake. They may say "z-z-z-z" in playing airplane, "ch-ch-ch" in playing train, or "r-r-r" in dramatizing "The Lion and the Mouse." These naturally isolated sounds are fun both to say and to hear, and the teacher may make use of them in listening games. She may use them in such manner as this: "This afternoon when you were rocking your dolly to sleep, Margaret, I saw you put your finger to your lips [demonstrating], and I heard you say something. Does anyone remember what Margaret said?" Suggest "sh" to the class. Then say, "Sometimes we hear that same sound when we talk. Can you hear it when I say *ship? shoe? sugar?* Did you hear it at the *beginning* or at the *end?* Can you hear it when I say *brush?* At the *beginning* or at the *end?* Can you hear the sound in *fishing?* Where did you hear it? Yes, in the *middle*." Ask the children to say as many words as they can think of that contain the same sound.

A pair of sounds that children can experiment with are the sounds at the beginning of *see* and the beginning of *zoo*. Let pupils first try to make the *s*-sound that a whistling teakettle or a steam radiator makes. This is the sound in words like *see, slow, faster, yes, sticks*. Then suggest that they keep their mouths in the position for the whistling teakettle but try to change the sound to the *z*-sound of a buzzing bee instead. All they need to do is to add voice to the *s*-sound. They can feel the change if they put a finger to their throats while they alternate the two sounds. The vocal sound feels like a little motor in the throat. The buzzing sound may also be suggested by an electric razor, or a door buzzer, or an airplane, or a large mosquito. This is the sound that can be heard in such words as *zoo, zebra, rose, easy, boys,* and *girls*. The children may discover for themselves that the *z*-sound is made like the *s*-sound except that "z-z-z" has a voiced sound vibrating in the throat.

Children may also enjoy making the *ch*-sound of a sneeze or of a train. This sound occurs in *chicken, children, marching, watch, catch*. It is also the sound at the end of the word *ouch*.

Listening for these sounds in words, trying to hear them at the beginning, middle, or end of a word, and trying to think of words that contain the sounds—these activities help children realize that language has the characteristic of duration in time and that sounds follow one another in sequence from the beginning to the end of a word.

THE WORD AS THE UNIT OF LANGUAGE

Notice that in all the suggestions made in this chapter for developing auditory skills, words are always pronounced as units. The children learn to hear within the total auditory impression of the words the beginning and ending sounds. The word is not broken up into separate sounds. Occasionally the teacher may say a word slowly, so that the word is drawled a bit, to enable the children to give better attention to the sequence of sounds. But even then, the sounds are not separated but blend naturally from one to the next. Occasionally the teacher, for emphasis on the beginning sound, may ask the children to get their lips or tongue *ready to say* the word without actually saying it, so that the children may "feel" how the word *begins*. The children are not asked to isolate the sound, however, and the word remains the *unit of language* in all the games and training exercises.

BIBLIOGRAPHY

Gardner, D. Bruce. "If Your Child Doesn't Listen—," *Today's Health*, 88 (March 1960), 14, 85, 87, 88. Describes the inconsistency and emotionality with which many parents speak to their children, explaining how this manner of speaking teaches children early in life to "tune out" what is being said. Also points out that in our society there is more status attached to speaking than to listening.

Murphy, George. "We Also Learn by Listening," *Elementary English*, 26 (March 1949), 127-128, 157. Suggests various listening experiences which are a natural part of the primary-grade child's experience.

Nichols, Ralph G., and Cashman, Paul H. "The Approval Factor in Listening," *Education*, 53 (January 1960), 268-271. Discusses the effect of adult (parent or teacher) attitudes toward listening on the listening attitudes developed by children.

Nichols, Ralph G., and Lewis, Thomas R. *Listening and Speaking*. Dubuque, Iowa: William C. Brown Co., 1954.

Discusses the growth of interest in listening as a skill, some of the early research in the field, false assumptions regarding listening, and ten components of effective listening. The discussion is directed at the adult level of listening, but the primary teacher may see ways of directing her instruction to the related areas at the beginning level.

Pronovost, Wilbert, and Kingman, Louise. *The Teaching of Speaking and Listening in the Elementary School.* New York: Longmans, Green and Co., 1959. Illustrative lessons demonstrate the part that listening plays in the development of oral language.

Russell, David H., and Russell, Elizabeth F. *Listening Aids Through the Grades: 190 Listening Activities.* New York: Teachers College, Columbia University, 1959. A collection of exercises, activities, and suggestions which a teacher may use in relation to a planned program in language arts.

Schwartz, Sheila. "What Is Listening?" *Elementary English,* 38 (April 1961), 221-224. Discusses listening as it functions in the classroom. Stresses the responsibility of the speaker (teacher) to say things in an interesting enough manner to motivate the audience (pupils) to listen.

Strickland, Ruth G. *The Language Arts in the Elementary School.* Boston: D. C. Heath and Co., 1957. Chapters 6 and 7 include discussions of the kinds of problems in listening that confront the first-grader.

Wachner, Clarence. " 'Listening' in an Integrated Language Arts Program," *Elementary English,* 33 (December 1956), 491-496. Discusses the relation of a person's experience to his capacity for critical listening.

Wepman, Joseph. "Auditory Discrimination, Speech, and Reading," *Elementary School Journal,* 60 (March 1960), 325-333. Research study of the relationship between auditory discrimination, accuracy of articulation, and reading.

_____. "The Interrelationship of Hearing, Speech and Reading," *The Reading Teacher,* 14 (March 1961), 245-247. Discusses hearing as a developmental process related to the process of learning to read.

Witty, Paul A., and Sizemore, Robert A. *Studies in Listening*. Champaign, Ill.: National Council of Teachers of English, 1958-1959. Review of research in listening at all grade levels. Provides background information relating to the need for planned listening instruction beginning at the kindergarten and first-grade levels. (Reprinted from *Elementary English*.)

chapter five

Pupils Use Their Eyes

It takes a great deal of experience in reading to acquire the visual skills of an expert reader. Fleet, rhythmical eye movements with a wide span of sensitivity to printed words on either side of the fixation point are acquired largely through the process of extensive reading. The eye is directed in its movements and pauses along the text according to the needs of the reader. When a reader needs to identify an unknown printed word, he will give careful scrutiny to its visual details, with many fixations of the eye back and forth along the line of printed letters. When he reaches a snag in the meaning, he may look back at each word to follow the thought more carefully. If he lacks sufficient proficiency in language to anticipate or complete a language pattern, he must bring each word into central vision, with a narrow span of recognition. As he learns to recognize an increasing number of printed words and develops increasing proficiency in language, his eye movements become more and more like those of the mature reader.

THE DEVELOPMENT OF EYE CONTROL

The ability to adjust the eyes for near vision begins to develop in early infancy. The gaze of the month-old infant is attracted by the window light or by the movement of a bright object. At two months of age, the infant is able to coordinate the two eyes so that he can follow a moving object with both of them. He is also able to fixate and respond to a human face.

At three months, the infant will look with interest at his own hand, and at four months, he is able to regard an object placed in his hand. He may also, when placed in a sitting position, fixate a small object placed on a table top. As he becomes able to reach for and manipulate objects, he fixates them as he holds them. From this time on, the child steadily develops the ability to bring his two eyes into adjustment at points near enough so that he can observe and thus better control his hand manipulation.

The challenge for a beginning reader

The five- or six-year-old child who is getting ready to read has new and exacting visual adjustments to make in preparation for reading. He must accustom his eyes to near-point vision for longer and longer periods. He must fuse the images of the two eyes for single vision under more exacting conditions than ever before. Although slight blurring of details or doubling of images may not have interfered greatly with the perception of the larger pictures and objects the child has been handling in his preschool life, they will interfere with the discrimination of the relatively small details of printed words. The child is called upon to make finer judgments of shape, size, place relationships, and arrangements of visual details than he has ever had to make before. And for almost the first time, unless he has already learned to read, he will need to direct his eyes in sequence from left to right.

Experience makes a difference

The visual abilities of five- and six-year-olds vary greatly
at the time of school entrance, partly because of physical
differences and partly because of the differing experiences
the children have had. Some children have developed habits
of careful observation and scrutiny of details. Others have
learned to react only to the gross visual differences among
objects in their environment. Those children who have
enjoyed many opportunities for interesting play with manipulative toys during their preschool life have, in most
cases, developed considerable ability to adjust their eyes
and hold their attention to close work. Children who have
lacked toys and equipment for manipulation are especially
in need of manipulative activities and experiences at school.

GAMES AND EXERCISES FOR DEVELOPING VISUAL SKILLS

All children can profit from games and exercises designed
to develop specific visual skills, although the amount and
nature of visual training needed is clearly related to the
kind of preschool experiences the child has had. The games
and exercises suggested in the following pages have been
designed to provide the teacher with a source of material
from which she can select according to her children's needs
at any given time. These games and exercises are presented
in five different groups: (1) activities for building a vocabulary of visual terms; (2) games and exercises for developing
the ability to make gross visual discriminations; (3) games
and exercises for developing the ability to compare and
contrast; (4) games and exercises for developing greater
sensitivity to specific visual qualities; (5) exercises for developing left-to-right eye movement.

Building a vocabulary of visual terms

Each classroom should be equipped with a shelf well sup-
plied with manipulative toys. These may include beads for
stringing, pictures for coloring, pegboards, blocks, scissors,
modeling clay, trains, picture puzzles, nested cubes, gradu-

ated towers, materials for sewing and weaving. As children play with these objects, the teacher will have an opportunity to use words that describe the visual qualities of the object the child is creating. She may refer to size or color. She may talk about place relationships or directions. She may compare and contrast two or more objects. She may use words that describe shape or indicate distance.

The activity of stringing beads might lead to the following use of visual descriptive terms: "What a pretty *blue* bead you are putting on your string, Albert. Which *color* are you going to choose next? Is this bead shaped *like a ball* or *like an egg?*"

Cutting out pictures suggests the following type of comment: "You are cutting very nicely, Billy. Now you need to go *around* the duck's head, then *straight across* his back."

Building blocks provide another type of situation: "What a *tall* tower you have built. It goes *up* and *up* and *up*. Can you put another block on the *top* and make it still *taller?*"

A pegboard gives a good opportunity for using the words *big* and *little* in a situation requiring comparison: "That's right, Jane. Put a *big* peg in a *big* hole, and a *little* peg in a *little* hole!"

Picture puzzles provide a variety of opportunities for using descriptive terms. A picture of a bus might lead to the following comments: "What shape is the piece that makes a wheel of the bus? Yes, it is called a *circle*. And the window that you look out of is a *square*."

Such comments will help the child learn the terms he will need to describe the visual qualities of other objects he sees. Children should also be encouraged to comment on each other's building and play activities, for this reinforces their learning of the terms they have heard the teacher use. Further group discussion will have a spiraling effect in vocabulary reinforcement.

Developing the ability to make gross visual discriminations

Before attempting to develop ability in making fine visual discriminations, make sure that the children can detect gross visual differences. Picture-matching games have great diagnostic value. For example, divide a large card into six or eight squares, or "boxes," and paste an attractively colored picture of some well-known object in each box. Next, prepare as many small cards as there are boxes, and paste duplicate pictures on the small cards. If printed pictures are not available, you can make simple line drawings that will serve the purpose just as well.

When the large card and the corresponding small cards are ready, mount them on an easel or on the ledge of the chalkboard. Indicate, by pointing, one of the objects on the large card and request a child to find the small card that shows the same thing. Pictures for such an activity might look like this:

If children have difficulty in matching such pictures of objects, with their widely assorted shapes and colors and details, they are probably not ready to make finer discriminations. If further practice with gross visual discrimination seems necessary, additional games of the same type may easily be prepared so that children who need such experiences may work for a few minutes each day to develop this basic skill. While children are working on games of this kind, the teacher will have a good opportunity to develop readiness for the skills of comparing and contrasting if she uses the terms *alike* and *different* in commenting on the pictures. She can also encourage the children to use the terms themselves, so that they will develop not only some skill in comparing but also a vocabulary for talking about comparisons.

Developing the ability to compare and contrast

Activities involving the comparing and contrasting of visual forms provide a good basis for further work in the development of visual skills. A game called "How are they different?" is a good starter for this kind of activity. The procedure is as follows:

Present two identical pictures and ask, "Are these pictures alike?" Agree that they are. Then say, "In what way do they look alike?" If children do not respond at once, start the discussion by saying, "This girl has a blue dress [pointing to one picture] and this girl's dress [pointing to the other picture] is blue, too." Comment on other details: "Both girls are *little*—they are the same *size;* they have the same *kind* of shoes, and their aprons are the same *shape*." Draw out as many similarities as the children are able to think of and add a few other details that the children may not have noticed.

Next, present one of these two pictures with another, this time a contrasting one. Ask, "Do these pictures look alike?" Agree that they are different and then ask, "How are they different?" Point out the differences—for example, "That one is a picture of a girl, while the other is a picture of a boy," or "The girl is little, while the boy is big." Draw out as many differences as children are able to think of. Through this type of comparison, detail by detail, children will grow accustomed to making careful scrutiny of all parts of a picture. At the same time, they will develop an increasing ability to give clear verbal expression to their observations.

Comparing pairs of objects may also provide helpful practice. A set of paired objects like the following might be prepared.

Some of the pairs should be alike, some different. Say, "Look at the pictures in each box. Tell me which boxes contain objects that are alike and which boxes contain objects that are different." Point successively at each box, giving various children a chance to answer.

An exercise involving slightly more difficult visual discrimination can be constructed by placing together pictures of objects that are generally similar but different in detail. A set of paired objects like the following might be used:

Ask children to identify the objects in the first box. Then ask, "How did you know which was the chicken?" Answers may include reference to feet, beak, or shape of head. Continue in a similar manner to ask for identifying details of church or school, of horse or cow, of car or truck, of table or desk.

Developing greater sensitivity to specific visual qualities

With a background of experience in the kinds of activities outlined in the preceding paragraphs, children should be able to advance into the more difficult area of developing sensitivity to specific visual qualities. These qualities include size, color, shape, position, and internal detail. Games and exercises such as the following may be used for developing skill in each of these areas.

Observing size. Nested cubes and graduated towers require accurate discrimination of size, and these toys are fun for five- and six-year-olds as well as for younger children. The nested cubes are self-correcting, because a larger cube cannot be fitted into a smaller one. The cubes may also be placed upside down upon each other to form a graduated tower with the largest cube at the bottom and the smallest at the top. Playing with the cubes calls attention to size and to size differences, and the activity provides a pleasant introduction to more difficult estimates of size relationships.

Wall charts like the one shown on page 100 may also be used for practice in recognizing the relative size of objects. Ask children to indicate in each row the larger (or the smaller) object. The exercise can be made increasingly difficult if each row of pictures is drawn nearer and nearer the same size.

The familiar story of "The Three Bears" provides an opportunity for making estimates of size. Children enjoy studying pictures of bowls, chairs, and beds of different sizes and picking out Baby Bear's bowl, or Mother Bear's chair, or Father Bear's bed.

Observing color. Written words are usually printed in black on white paper, so that reading does not generally require skill in color discrimination. Many reading-readiness books, however, do use color, and many instructional materials for young children require some kind of color discrimination. Thus a child who does not know color names, or who cannot discriminate the primary colors, is often handicapped in participating in pre-reading activities.

Color-matching games will help the teacher to find those pupils who have a weakness in color vision. If a pupil matches colors successfully but miscalls them, he needs help in learning the color names, but he probably has normal color vision. If, however, he matches green with red or brown, or shows other confusions in color matching, he may be color-blind. Almost 10 per cent of boys have weakness in color vision. Girls rarely have trouble with color. True color blindness is not usually considered remediable, although many efforts have been made in recent years to help the color blind. Teachers should recognize color-blind children and give them unobtrusive help in finding the right crayons. Otherwise they may make mistakes on the pages of their workbooks that require coloring even though they understand the directions.

In games for developing the names of colors and color discrimination, it is a good plan to call on the color-blind child for blue and yellow discriminations rather than for red or green. Most color-blind children can succeed in discriminating blue and yellow, for although we use the term "color blind," these children are really not blind to color—they simply do not differentiate certain colors, usually red and green. They receive definite color impressions, however, and they enjoy color and coloring within the range of their color sensitivity. Since color plays such a large part in the visual materials used in the beginning stages of instruction, help in learning names of colors and in making color discriminations is important.

Identification of color may be practiced first with a game called "Touch something yellow (or red, or blue, or green)." When a pupil has identified the desired color in some object in the classroom, he goes quietly to the object and touches the color. Other pupils do the same until no more yellow objects can be found. Another approach to the identification of color may be: "All children who are wearing something *blue* may *skip*." After these children have enjoyed a lively skip, let children who are wearing something red hop. Continue with other colors and other similar activities. Such games are fun and give most children an opportunity to participate a large part of the time, since most will be wearing several colors.

At this stage of color naming, many children will be asking for or using the names pink, lavender, and others besides the primary colors. Use these color names, too, and relate the color to a primary color if possible. *Pink* is *light red*, *lavender* is *light purple*, navy is *dark blue*. Find two shades of red and point out that one is darker or lighter than the other, but that both are *red*. Allow children to experiment with colors. "When we press a blue crayon hard, we make *dark blue*. When we press it gently, we make *light blue*." Overlap two colors when coloring with crayons and let the children discover that blue and yellow blend into green, red and yellow into orange, red and blue into violet.

Observing shape. Show children a number of interesting pictures, each having one central figure with a distinctive shape—a baby, a giraffe, a car, or some such item. Prepare outline drawings of the central figures in advance. An easy way to do this is to place an onionskin paper over the picture and trace the outline (simplifying details) with a black crayon. After the children have named the pictures, present the outline figures for identification. When the children succeed in identifying pictures of objects having widely differing outlines or contours, trace a number of animal pictures in the same way. The outline drawings of a sheep and a dog will require finer discrimination for identification than the outline drawings of a baby and a car. Whenever a child has difficulty in identifying an animal from its shape alone, let him look again at the original pictures and fit the tracing to the pictures until he discovers which animal was traced.

Most children enjoy making tracings themselves. Let children trace objects in magazine pictures—just the outlines with no internal detail. These traced outlines may then be thumbtacked to a board so that other pupils can try to identify the objects.

Silhouettes cut from black paper are fun too, especially at Halloween. Let children cut freehand into black paper, guided only by their concept of the shapes of pumpkins, witches, and brooms.

Playing with shadow forms also provides practice in discriminating shapes. Children love to create shadow bunnies, shadow faces, and shadow chickens by folding hands and moving fingers to cast shadows on a screen or on the wall. An artificial light source will probably be needed. A light that can be clamped onto a chair or table, or a gooseneck lamp, will make it possible to place the light at a useful angle for casting shadows in the desired direction. If a transluscent screen of some kind is available, children may present shadow figures from behind the screen, provided an adequate source of light can be set up behind them.

Cloud formations provide another interesting means of studying shapes. The teacher fortunate enough to have a classroom with a good view of the sky will find many occasions when cloud formations are vivid enough to stimulate children's imaginations. With a little encouragement, children will find all sorts of shapes in clouds—elephants and giants, horses and ships, toadstools and tigers.

In teaching children to observe characteristic shapes, attention needs to be called to certain basic forms such as circle, square, triangle, rectangle, oval, diamond. If these shapes are identified when they appear in pictures and they are called by their proper names, the names will become familiar to children through frequent repetition.

Further awareness of geometric forms may be developed by having children draw the forms themselves. Large forms, in simple outline, may be mounted on the chalkboard, or the teacher may simply draw the forms with chalk on the board. Children may then be encouraged to make these forms in the air using a large arm movement. This procedure may be followed by finger tracing on a large chart, after which children may try to draw their own geometric forms, using crayon and large sheets of newsprint. Such activities develop not only readiness for handwriting but also a heightened awareness of the characteristics of the form itself and a quicker and more assured response to its visual presentation. Encourage the children to name or draw as many objects as they can which have the same general shape as one of the basic forms. A circle, for example, may remind them of such familiar objects as a wheel, a doughnut, the sun, a button, a plate, and a pumpkin.

Picture puzzles provide another means of increasing sensitivity to form. Two pieces fit together if their edges match, but the shape of one piece must extend out where its mate is indented. Practice with this type of fitting extends the child's knowledge of space relationships. Another problem-solving procedure may also be used in completing a picture puzzle. The child may anticipate the proper outline of the object in the picture and seek the piece that provides this outline. Thinking about the puzzle in this way also strengthens awareness of the characteristics of various shapes.

Reading-readiness books usually contain many attractive pages designed to call attention to shape. The child is asked to mark the picture that is different in each row of pictures. The example shown on page 104 is representative of this type of page.

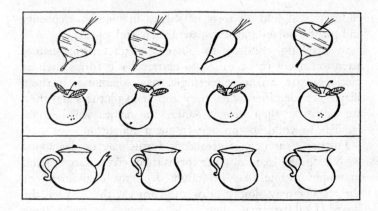

Observing position.   Many objects look alike in size, shape, and color but are placed in different positions with regard to the top, bottom, right, or left sides of the visual field. A number of printed letters are alike, too, except for their orientation or the way they are turned. The letter *u* looks like the letter *n,* for example, except that one is inverted when compared with the other. A *b* looks like a *d* and a *p* looks like a *q* except for the right and left reversal of the half circle with reference to the vertical. A *b* and *p* are different in the extension of the vertical above or below. In reading, the ability to distinguish orientation with reference to up, down, right, and left is an important skill.

Up and *down* are usually easily discriminated by five- and six-year-old children. Rarely will a child draw an object upside down on the chalkboard, where *up* is really "up" and *down* is "down." A few children may fail to recognize *up* and *down,* however, when they are drawing on a piece of paper that lies flat on the table. When they draw on paper laid flat, some children may regard each edge as a base and draw people with their feet planted against any or all of the four sides. Other children may consider the flat page as a kind of *floor* or *ground* and draw objects here and there like a map or floor plan without reference to any side as a base, since the entire paper is the base.

To help children to learn the concepts of *up* and *down* on a flat piece of paper, the teacher may sketch on the

chalkboard drawings similar to those in the illustration above. With one or more such drawings on the board, children may be encouraged to come up and show the class which boy is going *up* and which boy is going *down* the steps, or which plane is flying *up* and which plane is flying *down*. Then, giving the children a piece of drawing paper, the teacher may ask, "Which is the *top* of your paper? Which is the *bottom?*"

Concepts of *right* and *left* also need to be developed. Most children of five or six years are just in the midst of learning to distinguish between right and left. Some can identify their right and left hands, but some cannot. Three simple games and activities may help during this period to reinforce the right-left concept.

1. The singing game "Looby Loo," during which children alternately put their right and left hands "in" or "out" and give them a "shake, shake, shake," is a pleasant and practical way of teaching children to distinguish left from right. As children play the game, the teacher will have an opportunity to observe which children are having difficulty and which have mastered this concept.

2. A variation of "Looby Loo" may be used with some groups. Let the children make bracelets from strips of

brightly colored paper, with fringed edges for extra fun. The teacher may use paper clips or pressure tape to fasten the bracelets, making sure that each child is wearing his bracelet on his *right* arm. The "Looby Loo" game then proceeds as before, only this time each child knows that his *right* arm is the arm with the bracelet. As children "shake, shake, shake" their right hands, all the paper bracelets come up in unison, providing a further reinforcement for the concept of right and left.

3. The next step in the development of the right-left concept is its application to the scrutiny of two-dimensional representations. For practice at this level of difficulty, simple sketches of objects such as those in the illustration may

be used. Children may be asked to observe, first, which cup is different and which dog is different. Next, they may be asked to try to explain how these objects differ from the other objects in the row. If the terms *right* and *left* do not immediately come out in the discussion, the teacher may give the explanation, pointing out that one handle is on the left side, while the other two are on the right. Additional practice with similar rows of objects will give children an opportunity to add the terms *left* and *right* to their descriptions of objects they are scrutinizing.

In addition to the concepts *up* and *down*, *right* and *left*, there is the concept of relative position. An observer needs to be able to locate an object in reference to other objects in the same visual field. A lamp is *on* the table, *by* the chair, *before* the fireplace. As children describe what they see in a picture, they can be encouraged to phrase the description in terms of space relationships. The child may say, for example, "The boy is *on* the pony," or "The eggs are *in* the nest," or "The clock is *between* the candlesticks." Children often enjoy describing a constantly enlarging space as in the old song: "The bird was in the egg, the egg was in the nest, the nest was in the tree, the tree was in the field, and the green grass grew all around, all around." Concepts of space beyond the immediate visual field may be developed with a paraphrase of the song such as the following: "The chalk is in the box, the box is on the desk, the desk is on the floor, the floor is in the room, the room is in the school, the school is in Our Town, Our Town is in Our State, Our State is in the United States, the United States is in the world." A knowledgeable youngster may want to go on still further by adding "and the world is in space."

Observing internal details. Many objects have the same shape, size, color, and position but have slight differences in detail. For example, two cups may resemble each other in every way except that one is decorated with a narrow stripe and the other is decorated with a broader one. Two houses may be alike except that one has just one window by the door and the other has two windows. Two pumpkin faces may be alike except that one has a round hole and the other a triangular hole for the nose. These slightly different details are often lost in the general impression of similarity. It requires careful scrutiny and comparison, item by item, to detect slight differences of detail, yet many printed words differ only in a single small detail. The word *hand* is shaped much like *band* and *hard:* a short added line closing the bottom of the first letter in *hand* will change the word to *band;* an erasure of the right-hand vertical stroke in the letter *n* will cause the word *hand* to become *hard.*

Practice in careful observation of small details accustoms children to notice slight differences and prepares them for the fine visual scrutiny that will be necessary in discriminating printed words.

Developing left-to-right eye movement

Most of the pre-reading materials on the market provide opportunities for habituating the child to move his eyes from the left toward the right. In picture stories children begin with the upper left-hand picture, which is the first episode, and continue toward the right to the next episode. In pages on which pictures are used for developing auditory or visual discrimination, the teacher may name the objects in left-to-right order, and children may be encouraged to scrutinize them and respond to them in that order. Combining eye movement with hand movement from left to right helps a child reinforce the habit of moving from left to right. For example, a large picture showing a dog at the extreme left and a doghouse at the extreme right provides the child with an opportunity to show with his finger or with a crayon the path the dog takes to the doghouse. Practice, as needed, may easily be provided at the chalkboard or at the children's seats, where they can use crayon and large pieces of newsprint. Children will delight in drawing their own representations of dog and doghouse and, guided by the teacher's demonstration, will show with a sweep of hand or crayon, from left to right, how the dog ran straight into his house.

ADJUSTING VISUAL TRAINING ACTIVITIES TO THE CHILD

The eye-training games and exercises described in this chapter are inherently attractive and interesting to little children. There is the element of puzzle in visual games, the pride of success when the puzzle is solved, and the constant allure of attractive pictures and objects. Little children are eye-hungry, and there is seldom a time when the teacher says "Look" that eyes do not turn at once to see. She may say "Listen" a time or two in vain before she gains the attention of the class, but not "Look."

Making use of the children's natural interest in all they see and helping them develop in visual skill should be a joyous experience for the teacher as well as for the child. Any game, however, can be spoiled if too much pressure is placed on the outcome. When children have difficulty in making a discrimination, the teacher should look for possible reasons for the difficulty and perhaps try material where simpler discriminations are to be made. Games should be constantly adjusted to the child, in an attempt always to achieve that desirable state where the material presented is easy enough for success but challenging enough to provoke careful thinking. Success should not be empty but filled with a glow of self-approval, confidence in one's ability, and eagerness for another experience.

BIBLIOGRAPHY

Blum, Henrik L.; Peters, Henry B.; and Bettman, Jerome W. *Vision Screening for Elementary Schools.* Berkeley: University of California Press, 1959. Reports a comprehensive investigation designed to develop a visual-screening program for use in the average school system.

Dvorine, Israel. "What You Should Know About Sight," *Education,* 78 (April 1958), 471-475. A nontechnical explanation of the function of the eye in normal vision.

Gesell, Arnold; Ilg, Francis L.; and Bullis, Glenna E. *Vision: Its Development in Infant and Child.* New York: Paul B. Hoeber, Inc., 1949. A systematic investigation of the visual function from birth to age ten. Comparisons of visual function are made from age to age and from child to child. The primary emphasis is on the normal aspects of visual development.

Goins, Jean Turner. *Visual Perceptual Abilities and Early Reading Progress* (Supplementary Educational Monographs, No. 87). Chicago: University of Chicago Press, 1958. Investigates two problems: (1) Does visual training produce an increase in reading ability at the first-grade level? (2) Is performance on visual-perceptual tests at the beginning of Grade 1 related to success in reading at the end of the first year?

Robinson, Helen M. "Visual Screening Tests for Schools," *Elementary School Journal,* 54 (December 1953), 217-222.

Provides information about the relative reliability, usability, and cost of visual screening tests that may be used for school purposes.

Vetterli, Clarence H. "How Good is 20/20 Vision?" *Education*, 80 (September 1959), 41-45. Discusses the dangers in using the Snellen Chart as a vision screening test.

chapter six

Reading
Is
Interpreting

A third-grade teacher asked a pupil to read a passage aloud. He did so, quickly and easily, without an error in pronunciation. "That was fine, Howard," commented the teacher. "Now close your book and tell us, in your own words, just what the passage was about."

"Why . . . why . . . ," faltered the boy, "you just asked me to *read* it. I didn't pay any attention to what it *said!*"

Children like Howard who read mechanically but fail to get the meaning do not enjoy reading. They cannot use reading; they have trouble concentrating for long on a process so empty of meaning. Mere word calling without understanding must be dull and dreary, indeed. Yet children can be found in our middle and upper grades who recite the words of the text in a docile and polite manner but have little idea about the content. In many cases this is because teachers have felt that their responsibility ended with teaching a child to attach the proper sounds to printed words. They have left it to the child to figure out as best he can what the text means. Too often the results have been disastrous. If reading is to serve any purpose, the child must learn to *interpret* what he reads. This interpretation becomes the heart of reading and, as such, should be a central part of developing reading readiness.

THE FOUR COMPONENTS OF THE TOTAL READING PROCESS

The act of reading is so familiar to adults that they often lose sight of what is involved in the process. The experienced adult reader instantly associates meaning with most of the words he sees as his eyes move along the printed lines. These meanings as a rule approximate those the author had in mind when he wrote the words. In associating meanings with words, the reader fuses these meanings into thought units until he understands the ideas the author has expressed. He reacts to these ideas and integrates them with his own. In this total reading process then there may be distinguished four components: (1) word perception, (2) comprehension of the ideas represented by the words, (3) reaction to these ideas, and (4) assimilation or integration of the ideas with previous knowledge or experience. Although these four aspects of the reading process occur almost simultaneously, each one needs to receive careful attention during the early stages of learning to read.

Word perception

For both children and adults, *word perception* is the first step in interpreting printed language. Word perception involves identifying the printed symbol and associating it with the spoken word for which that symbol stands. A detailed explanation of the process of word perception may be found in *On Their Own in Reading*, by William S. Gray.[1]

[1] William S. Gray, *On Their Own in Reading*, Revised. Chicago: Scott, Foresman and Company, 1960.

Comprehension

Comprehension of the ideas expressed is the second step in interpreting printed language. This involves determining the meanings of words in their language settings and at the same time linking these meanings into larger language patterns and fusing them into a chain of related ideas.

The reader who comprehends fully projects himself into the situation as he reads. He shares the author's moods and emotions and creates vivid sensory imagery. For example, he not only learns *about* the desert; he experiences it. He sees the limitless expanses of sand and more sand; he hears the whine of the wind as it moves over the empty stretches, and he struggles to walk against it; he feels the sting of the sand on his face and body, the burning heat, and the thirst that catches and dries his throat; and he suffers with the characters in the story as they search for some kind of habitation. For a time, this reader actually *lives* in the desert.

Reaction

The thoughtful reader not only shares experiences, but *reacts* to them. He reacts to the ideas and to the characters, either intellectually or emotionally, or both. Intellectually, he decides whether the facts are accurate or not; whether he has found the information he was seeking; whether he approves or disapproves of the ideas. Emotionally, he decides whether he likes or dislikes the actions and the characters that perform them; he may feel antipathy for one, sympathy and kinship for another. He may reject the action of one character as ignoble, stupid, or cruel; he may approve the action of another as being selfless or courageous. The reader decides whether he likes the style and content of a story and, through his intellectual and emotional reactions, decides whether he will accept or reject the author's thesis.

Assimilation

The fullest interpretation is found in the assimilation or integration of ideas with the reader's total experience. Some ideas are merely organized with others of like kind to add to knowledge. Other ideas may serve as a basis for guiding activities—they direct the reader in what to do and how to do it. Still other ideas may require widespread reorganization of previous ideas to resolve conflicts. This fusion of new ideas with existing ideas is possibly the most significant component of the total reading act.

All these degrees of interpretation—word perception, comprehension, reaction, and assimilation—are successively dependent upon one another. Each is important to the next and to the whole process. Comprehension of meaning can come about only if the reader accurately perceives the verbal symbols that represent the author's meaning. And, in turn, valid reactions to and full integration of the ideas can come about only if the reader accurately comprehends the meaning of the text. A child who learns from his very first contact with printed words to interpret the text thoughtfully will find increasing value and satisfaction with each successive stage of growth in reading.

DEVELOPING INTERPRETATIVE SKILLS AT THE PRE-READING LEVEL

At the pre-reading level pictures, stories, and experiences take the place of a printed text, but the thinking processes of interpretation are much the same as the child will use later when he actually reads. This chapter, then, is concerned with interpretation as related to the reading-readiness program, and the games and exercises described are designed to help pre-reading children develop the specific kinds of thinking that they will need to interpret pre-primer stories.

Pictures as well as words derive their meanings from the child's ability to bring to mind relevant associations. At the pre-reading level, as at succeeding levels of reading, a child can interpret content only by relating that content to previous experience that he remembers and can verbalize. Verbalization in turn requires a certain mastery of oral language. Children need to be able to put their own ideas into words and to extract meaning from the spoken language they hear. Without this ability in speaking and listening they are handicapped in all kinds of verbal thinking and verbal response.

In varying degrees all children coming to school face the problem of developing their speaking and listening skills. They need to learn to associate meaning with many new words they have not heard before and to strengthen their familiarity with these words by incorporating them into their own speech patterns. Words so learned will be easily read for meaning when the time comes to associate oral with printed language.

One of the first steps in getting ready to interpret printed language, therefore, is developing the ability to interpret oral language.

Encouraging oral expression

A child cannot grow in any skill unless he has the desire and the opportunity to practice the skill. The following suggestions may provide the teacher with a variety of avenues for opening up opportunities for children to practice putting their thoughts into words.

A "news" period. A favorite group activity which stimulates spontaneous expression is the "news" period, in which children are encouraged to tell anything interesting that has recently happened to them. Bringing an object from home to school to show the group is especially helpful to the child who has difficulty in expression. Eyes are focused on the object he holds instead of on him, and if the child cannot manage to say anything, he may be helped by friendly questions from the group—"What is it?" "Where did you get it?" "What is it for?" Other children may be interested and have something to say about it too. The inexpressive child who holds the object gains confidence by standing before the group and having the honor of contributing the subject of discussion. He may later be able to repeat to an absentee some of what was said.

Shared experiences. Various types of shared experiences may serve as a point of departure in discovering the various interests of children. A science table and picture corner are helpful in stimulating discussion of objects that are of interest to the class. Trips and excursions may also provide a basis for discussion of a shared experience. Even the most inexpressive child may make some verbal contribution to the group activity when something interesting to him is being discussed.

Small groups. It is sometimes desirable to form a small group of those children who have the least ability to express themselves verbally. Games in which each child repeats some chant may accustom unresponsive children to hearing their own voices in the group. "Button, button, who has the button?" is an example of such a game. A special trip to the science table or picture corner in a small group apart from the more talkative children may give those who are shy or who lack verbal fluency a chance to express their ideas.

Artistic activities. Many children who cannot express themselves well in language can find an outlet for their ideas and feelings in drawing, painting, clay modeling, building, dramatic play, and other artistic expressions. They may not be able to *tell* what happened on an excursion, but they may be able to draw or model something they saw. They may not be able to *say* much about a pet duck brought to school, but they may be able to walk and quack like one. Praise for these nonlanguage types of expression will give a child a feeling of security and of contributing to the group; and this kind of experience may encourage him later to venture a few words when he finds himself capable of doing so.

Story hour. There is no more loved language activity in the kindergarten and first grade than the story hour. Picture books are especially helpful. As children study the bright pictures and identify the objects and actions portrayed, the text on each page should be read and reread until the child knows the story and then can take the book to his table, study the pictures, and recall almost verbatim the language of the text. As he repeats certain remembered words and phrases, he sees new meanings for these language patterns in the light of his further picture study.

Listening to one interesting story after another, both with pictures and without, and following each story with a guided discussion provides perhaps the best single activity through which language meanings may develop in the classroom. Excursions and visual aids to reinforce meanings should not be neglected when needed. Stories with continuous repetition of a phrase or refrain are especially helpful. Poems and jingles that tickle the ear are remembered almost at once, and they will sing again in children's minds until the language patterns become a part of the children's language meanings, to be used when needed.[2]

Learning to tell a story. Children should have an opportunity not only to hear stories but to tell their own. Pictures that portray an interesting incident are especially helpful in developing the ability to tell a story, because the idea is presented in the picture and the child needs only to formulate in language what he can understand of the pictured episode.

Children who can only name the objects they see in a picture may learn to add a descriptive term to the name. For example, if a child merely says, "A dog and a boy and a ball," the teacher can suggest that the dog is tiny, or black and white, or funny—that he is jumping, running, or barking; that the boy is little; that the ball is round and red and can bounce or roll. Then she can help the child to name the objects again as "A tiny black-and-white dog, a little boy, and a red ball" or "The dog is jumping, and the boy is running, and the ball is bouncing." Accepting this "story" about a picture with warm praise is important,

[2] See May Hill Arbuthnot, *Time for Poetry* (School Edition, Revised; Chicago: Scott, Foresman and Company, 1959), an anthology for teachers, and the accompanying record album, *Poetry Time.*

since it is a step to a higher level of verbal expression on the part of a child who heretofore has only named the objects in a picture.

Children who can give descriptions should next be led to see the objects in relationship to one another, not in isolation. The teacher may help the child who says, "It's about a little boy and a tiny black-and-white dog and a red ball," to see what the objects mean to each other. She can say, "The little boy has a tiny black-and-white dog. The dog is playing with the red ball." Or better, "The boy and his little black-and-white dog are playing with the red ball."

Children who can interpret objects in relationship to one another may be led one step further to understand the action in terms of the past or the future, or both. A narrative story may be developed by these children as they say, "A little boy brought his ball out into the yard to play. His tiny black-and-white dog wanted to play, too, so the boy is throwing the ball to him." Or the outcome of the pictured story may be anticipated by questions about what will happen next. "Will the dog bring the ball back to the boy, do you think?" The story may be concluded by a statement about the outcome, "The little dog ran to get the ball and brought it back to the boy."

A few children may be ready to understand a still higher level of interpretation—the evaluation of the story in a sort of "moral" or conclusion, such as "Dogs are good pets for a boy" or "Dogs can bring us things—like a newspaper —and help us." This helps the child to relate the pictured episode to his own life situation, calling to mind, perhaps, the fun he has had with his own pet. The teacher or one of the children may finally make a generalized statement covering the ideas elicited from the group.

Using episodic pictures. Narrative stories may be stimulated also by pictures of episodes arranged in sequence, like comic strips. Let the children tell a "what-is-happening" type of story for each episode and then anticipate what the outcome will probably be. With the pictures removed, allow the children to relate the entire story.

The following pictures are examples of two-step and four-step sequences:

Help children infer what is happening between two episodes. For example, in the four step sequence, suggest between the second and third pictures, "The family drove and drove until they came to a park." Anticipate with the children that the family will pick up and throw into the disposal baskets all of their waste paper and garbage so that the park will be clean and attractive for the next people who come to picnic. Generalize with children about the uses of parks, values of outdoor fun, and other possible conclusions. With pictures removed, let the children attempt to retell the entire story.

Narrating without the help of pictures. Retelling the stories heard in the story hour is the next higher level of language activity. Without pictures as guides, the child now must narrate the story from his own recall of the sequence of events. The ability to listen to a story of several episodes and then retell it accurately indicates a high level in organizing ideas and expressing them verbally. Too often teachers expect children to be able to achieve this level of proficiency almost immediately after hearing a story. A few five- and six-year-old children who have had superior and enriched language experiences may be able to do so, but the majority of children of these ages will profit from a carefully designed language program which begins at a simpler level and increases in difficulty in harmony with the children's growth.

Importance of a warm, friendly atmosphere. Urging a child to talk may only add emotional tension to his basic language difficulties. Any small effort he makes should be accepted. Attention should be directed to the idea the child is expressing, not to the child himself. Certainly, at this stage, it should not be directed to any deficiency in his language or speech. Growth in language takes place most rapidly in a permissive atmosphere of warm friendliness, in which each child is accepted as he is and thus feels free to be himself. The teacher watches for those activities in which the child talks most freely at his own level of language development. She then helps the child to develop his language further by giving him practice in talking and by providing language

models in her replies to him, gearing those replies to the
child's own level of understanding. The more familiar a
child is with language—the more language patterns he has
heard, understood, and used—the more readily he will think
in language symbols.

Developing experiential background

Along with practice in using language, children need an
opportunity to build up a background of concepts and
understandings based on direct experience. The greatest
degree of success will come in the early stages of reading
if the first stories the child reads present situations not too
different from those which he himself has already become
familiar with through direct participation. The pre-reading
period is the time during which the teacher can help children to build up this needed background. If some children
seem to lack experience for understanding the stories that
the teacher knows will soon be coming, she may be able
to provide opportunities for developing some of these
needed concepts. Several methods may be used.

Trips and excursions. Many children, especially in large
urban communities, do not have an opportunity to visit
places of interest in their own cities. Their experiences are
circumscribed by the narrow limits of their own neighborhood, with little or no contact with the outside world.
Thus when they come to school they find themselves confronted with pictures and stories that are meaningless to
them because they have had no experiences they can use as
a background for understanding. For these children, trips
to places where they may actually see a cow, a boat, a
train, a big store, a zoo, a barn, will be a great help in
building correct concepts.

Visual aids. Not all of the experiences children should
have may be available in every community. To make up
for the direct experiences which the community cannot
provide, a variety of visual aids may be used—pictures,

filmstrips, films. Care needs to be taken, however, when pictures are used to provide a background of information which is fairly complete. Pictures "out of context" may be as misleading to a child as words out of context may be for an adult. For example, in a slum area of a large city where most children had never seen a cow, a first-grade teacher tried to explain about cows, their habits, and their usefulness. On the chalk ledge she placed a picture of a cow, to which she referred from time to time. At the end of the discussion, one pupil gave an excellent summary of the facts. He told that cows live on farms, sleep in barns, give milk, moo, and eat grass. But when a classmate asked how big a cow was, he was perplexed for a moment. Then, carefully observing the size of the pictured cow, he answered, "Cows are about as big as a kitten." This child, in spite of all the information he had acquired about cows, had been given no way to know one very important fact about the animal. This pupil would obviously have a difficult time understanding a story about the experiences of a little girl who was afraid to go into a cow pasture, or of a family that got all of its milk from one cow.

Stories about people.   Stories about people and activities not within the pupil's personal experience are a source for developing concepts too. A child who has no father, for example, may listen avidly to stories in which he can develop concepts about fathers and what they do. A child whose parents quarrel and whose home life is rife with tensions and insecurities may discover through stories that there are peaceful and wholesome family interrelationships and that there are other ways to meet problems than through strife.

Developing thinking habits that facilitate interpretative skills

In addition to language and concept background, a child needs to develop certain types of thinking habits as a basis for learning to interpret printed language. The most impor-

tant of these thinking habits are: (1) the habit of giving
and maintaining attention to a specific problem or goal;
(2) the habit of verbalizing ideas; (3) the habit of creating
vivid sensory images; (4) the habit of organizing ideas;
(5) the habit of inferring motives and feelings of characters;
(6) the habit of using various kinds of clues for remembering the sequence of events, relationships, details of
description; and (7) the habit of evaluating.

Giving and maintaining attention.   One of the normal characteristics of little children is their distractibility. The more
immature children in a group display this trait more conspicuously than those of somewhat greater mental maturity.
The constant urge to twist and wiggle that characterizes
five- and six-year-olds is probably a reflection, in motor
activity, of the same need for constant change that children
demonstrate with regard to mental activity.

Recognizing that it is difficult for little children to remain
attentive for very long, but that the child who can do so
has an advantage in learning, the teacher tries to adjust to
this natural distractibility and at the same time, to foster
growth in attentiveness without pressure. She accepts the
child's need for frequent change and arranges her schedule
for brief periods of any one activity. Often more can be
accomplished in two ten- or fifteen-minute sessions than
in one twenty- or thirty-minute session. She permits wig-
gling and twisting because trying to hold still takes conscious effort on the part of a child and may therefore
distract him. She studies the interests of her pupils and
links details of the stories with their special interests and
motives. She strives for relaxed and happy relationships
among the children and between them and herself. She
helps the distractible child not by scolding but by praise
at a moment when she finds him particularly attentive, so
that he will know what giving attention means. Above all,
the teacher herself gives a good example of attention. A
teacher who looks attentively into the eyes of a child who
is talking, listens closely to what he is saying, tries to understand his exact meaning, however poorly phrased, and gives
him the most thoughtful reply of which she is capable will

hold that child's attention better than any device that can be suggested.

Verbalizing ideas. The habit of organizing ideas into acceptable language patterns is important as a basis for comprehending printed language. We comprehend what we read only insofar as we understand the language patterns represented by the printed text. For this reason the child who is advanced in language ability and who uses language easily to express his thoughts tends to comprehend and interpret printed language more easily than the child whose verbal skill is limited. Various ways of developing language ability were discussed earlier in this chapter (pp. 116-121).

Creating vivid sensory images. The ability to create a vivid memory image depends on how carefully one has observed the details of the original sensory impression. Careful observation of details depends in turn on a certain familiarity with the kinds of details which may be observed. Children can listen to sounds more discriminatingly, can think about them, and can describe them verbally when they know what some of the characteristics of sounds are. (Development of an understanding of the characteristics of sounds was described in Chapter 4.) They can respond more discriminatingly to visual stimuli when they understand and can verbalize some of the aspects of shape, size, color, and position. (Development of these understandings is traced in Chapter 5.) In addition to basic auditory and visual training, a number of special techniques may be used to help children form accurate and detailed visual and auditory images.

Activities: visual images. A number of interesting activities help children form accurate and detailed visual images. Display a picture for a few moments and have the children study the details. Then, with the picture removed, let the children discuss the picture story. This discussion is based on the memory image of the picture. The picture may be displayed and removed again several times to help those children who lose the image too soon or to settle a controversial point, such as whether the boy was pulling a two-wheeled cart or a four-wheeled wagon.

For about ten seconds expose a card containing a simple figure, such as a square with a dot in the middle, two circles connected by a short line, or some other form which the children can easily draw. Remove the card and let the children draw the figure from their memory image. Or, to vary the activity, take a child's hand and move it in the air to make a circle, square, or cross, and then let him go to the board and draw the pattern he visualized.

Have a child close his eyes and point to the clock, the door, the teacher's desk, the flag, the vase of flowers, or any other object in the room. Have him open his eyes after each pointing and check to see how accurately he has visualized the position of the object with reference to himself. The entire class could close their eyes and play this game together. It is easy to tell, by observing the pointing hands, which children have difficulty.

Let the children carefully observe several objects placed on a table, and then cover the objects with a cloth. Let the children try to visualize the objects under the cloth and tell what object is under each little hump. To vary this game, reach under the cloth and remove one object without letting the children see which one is gone. Then rearrange the others, uncover the pile, and ask what object is missing.

Activities: auditory images. Accurate auditory images are important for reading. Names of characters are recalled chiefly through the sound image of the name as pronounced. Even adults have difficulty identifying a character in a novel if the name is one they find difficult to pronounce. Children easily form auditory images of names that rhyme, such as Turkey-Lurkey, Henny-Penny, Piggy-Wig; or names that contain alliteration, such as Little Miss Muffet, Simple Simon, Dr. Doolittle, and other ear-ticklers.

Participating in roll call is enjoyable for children and may help them learn to remember names. Allow children to take turns in naming the pupils at their table or in their row and in deciding if anyone is absent. Ability to hold in mind a clear-cut auditory image of a person's name, to associate the name with the individual, and to recall the name thereafter is a skill many adults wish they had developed as children.

A whispering game is highly amusing and helps auditory accuracy at the same time. Whisper in the ear of one child a sentence such as, "A father took his little boy for a walk in the park every Sunday." Let him whisper the sentence to his neighbor and so on around a circle of six or eight children. The last child repeats the sentence aloud. Many changes in the sentence may take place in this game, to the amusement of the class. It takes precise auditory imagery to relay such a sentence accurately.

Two other games valuable for developing sound images are the tapping game "Echo," in which one child makes a series of irregular taps in imitation of those made by another child, and the game described on page 75, in which three sounds are given in sequence (ringing a bell, tapping on the table, shaking a rattle) and the child tells what was done *first, last,* or *in the middle.*

Give the first and last words with which a well-known jingle begins and let the children think of the words between: "Jack . . . nimble"; "Old . . . Hubbard"; "Pease . . . hot"; "Peter . . . eater"; "Mary . . . lamb"; "Simple . . . pieman." A child can scarcely succeed with this game unless he hears in his mind the entire refrain. Then let the child try to give the first and last words of the beginnings of other jingles. After giving the first word, he must think the ones in between until he comes to the last word, which he says. Encourage the children not to whisper or articulate the missing words but "just *think* how they sound." Counting by skipping every other number, "*One* (thinking two) *three* (thinking four) *five*, etc.," will stimulate auditory imagery of the skipped number.

The game of "Restaurant" is fun and helps develop visual as well as auditory memory images. First, have the children cut out from magazines colored pictures of breads, pies, cakes, fruits, vegetables, and meat dishes. These are placed on a table over which a "cook" presides. Three or four children, the customers, sit around another small table which may be set with paper plates, knives, forks, and spoons that have been designed, cut out, and colored by members of the class. Before taking their seats, the customers look over the cook's display. Another child, chosen as waiter, takes each customer's order and then repeats the orders to the cook. The cook places the appropriate pictures on a tray; the waiter carries it to the table and properly distributes the orders. As various children play waiter, and learn to remember which food each child has ordered, the lists can be increased by allowing the customers to order two items each or by enlarging the group at the table. This game serves many purposes. In addition to stimulating imagery, it can teach vocabulary (many children do not know the names of foods), classification (the cook may place together meats, vegetables, fruits, desserts), table setting (with right-left positions of knife, fork, and spoon), and concepts of how to order a meal and how to behave in a restaurant.

Creating sensory images while listening. Children need practice in visualizing the places and the people in stories they hear. Especially do they need to be encouraged to build up their own mental pictures, relying primarily on their own imaginations rather than on the pictures already provided by the illustrator of the book. If they develop their own mental images, they can then enjoy the process of comparing the pictures they have made in their minds with the illustrations the artist has created. Children who are saturated with prefabricated television pictures and with profusely illustrated picture books need to be encouraged and directed in developing and respecting their own imaginative creations. The fact that different people may have different pictures of the same character may be brought out, emphasizing that each person has his own private world of mental pictures and that each is to be respected, as long as it is appropriate to the facts of the story.

Another challenge to the child's imagination while he listens to a story is that of altering his mental image of a character in harmony with the passage of time or the changing of the social milieu. Since both concepts—time and social differences—are remote to most children, some special help and guidance may be needed in this aspect of story interpretation. One child, hearing the story of *Sleeping Beauty*, was so intrigued with his image of the baby princess at the beginning of the story that he lost track of the action for a while. When the story ended and the children were discussing it, he said, "There's just one thing I want to know. What ever happened to the baby?" His image of the baby had not grown up into the princess to correspond with the passage of time in the story. Similar problems may arise with characters who are introduced as poor, ragged, and unkempt and then, through natural or supernatural means, grow rich, beautiful, and famous. The child's mental picture may not change as easily as the fortunes of the character.

Most kindergartens and first grades have rest periods, when children can put their heads down on the tops of their tables or desks or actually lie down on small rugs for more complete relaxation. Occasionally during such a period when the children's eyes are closed, the teacher may suggest pleasant, drowsy images that help the pupils relax. "Pretend that your head is very heavy and that your arms are so limp they feel like water . . . Pretend you are seeing fluffy clouds float by—clouds that look like white boats on blue waves . . . Pretend a little bird is singing to you in notes as clear as a silver bell . . . Pretend you are lying on the sunny, warm, white sand by the ocean . . . Pretend you are in a garden of flowers and are holding a velvety red rose up to your face, its soft petals touching your cheek, your nose nuzzled into its heart . . . Pretend . . . pretend . . . pretend . . . ." Such images are dream stuff and, when suggested by language patterns, not only aid relaxation but accustom children to form sensory images in response to language.

Organizing ideas.   In order to organize ideas effectively for interpretation, the child must have in mind what he wants to find out. Questions asked by the teacher will help him to organize his thinking. "What do you think _____ will do next? Is he the kind of boy who would help his little sister? Did he help her in another story?" At the pre-reading level picture sequences, stories read aloud, and life experiences are interpreted in much the same way that printed text will be interpreted after the child begins actual reading.

Another of the skills children need to learn in order to be able to organize ideas effectively is the skill of identifying story characters. A frequent review of stories is helpful for the specific purpose of identifying characters with reference to their actions. The game "Who did it?" is fun. The teacher should ask such questions as: "Who huffed and puffed until he blew down a little straw house?" "Who ran away from a little old lady and a little old man?" "Who fell asleep in a little bear's bed?" This game is a good review of familiar stories and their characters, and it gives an extra purpose for remembering characters and events in new stories.

Among the first words a child will learn to read in a pre-primer are the names of story characters, and so the reading-readiness book should familiarize the children with these particular names in advance. If the boy pictured in the reading-readiness book is the same boy and has the same name that will be found in the pre-primer for example, then learning to read his name in the pre-primer will require only giving attention to the printed word form and making the association; children will already have used the name orally often enough to have a clear-cut auditory image of it. They will also know what kind of boy the name belongs to from their experiences with the picture-stories they have already read.

Inferring motives and feelings of characters. Storybook children, like real children, have reasons for their actions. What they do and what they say depend on their moods, their emotions, their personalities. Thus, in reading picture-stories of everyday life children may learn to infer, from the kind of person a character is, how he may behave in a particular situation. For example, a picture may show a boy with ball and bat approaching a dog. Children may be encouraged to consider what they know about this particular boy from previous stories—whether he is kind or cruel, friendly or unfriendly. After a discussion of his personality, they may be able to suggest what the boy is most likely to do next in the story—whether he will threaten the dog with the baseball bat or toss him the ball for a game of catch.

Animal stories, too, provide opportunities for inferring motives and anticipating outcomes. When children look at a picture or hear a story of a big bad wolf and a little pig, it is not hard for them to infer what the wolf's motives are, or how easy it would be for an innocent little pig to be taken in by his schemes. Appreciation of the situation makes their eyes grow round with suspense, and joyful relief comes when the little pig gets away.

The ability to size up a situation and anticipate the outcome in the light of the action, motives, and feelings of the characters can be fostered in picture work such as the following.

Say, "Look at the big picture. Then look at the two little pictures. Mark the one that shows what you think the boy in the big picture will do."

Say, "Look at the big picture. We can't see the little girl's face in the big picture, but mark the little picture that shows how you think she looks and feels."

After the children have finished, suggest an explanation for why they marked the pictures as they did. Ask them, also, to think what the characters in each of the pictures may be saying. The boy for instance might say, "Now don't fall out of your nest again." Or the girl might say, "Stop, you bad dog! Bring my doll back!"

Using clues for remembering.   Although young children learn quickly, they forget quickly, too, as many new experiences crowd into their active lives. "Yesterday" is a long time ago to a six-year-old. The teacher who gives attention to the process of remembering can contribute substantially to the efficiency of learning. Three aspects of the process may be emphasized at the pre-reading level: (1) observing carefully, (2) forming associations, and (3) perceiving relationships. Typical of the kind of material which may be used to develop skill in these areas is the page from a reading-readiness text reproduced below.[3] In using this page, the teacher may ask first, "Do you put away your toys when you finish playing?" In connection with the answers to this question she may point out the places in the classroom for putting away toys. This may lead to a discussion of *highest* and *lowest* shelves, or to *top*, *middle*, or *bottom* shelf. As pupils learn these terms they

[3] Helen M. Robinson, Marion Monroe, and A. Sterl Artley, *We Read Pictures*, with W. Cabell Greet, Linguistic Advisor (Chicago: Scott, Foresman and Company, 1962).

develop a sense of the *relationship* of one shelf to another, together with a stock of terms which they can use to express verbally their observations of such relationships.

Next, discussion may be led to the action in the picture. The teacher may ask: "Who is at the tail end of the parade?" "Who is in the middle?" "Who is leading the parade?" As in the discussion of shelves, pupils will learn to observe relationships—this time among characters—and the terms for expressing those relationships.

Pupils may then be led to *associate* the toys with the characters. Such questions as the following will encourage thinking about the relationships among toys and characters: "Have you seen the toys on the bottom shelf before?" "Who was playing with them?" "What is the toy that Sally is carrying?" "Have you seen the things on the middle shelf before?" "Who was playing with them?" "What is Jane carrying?" "Have you seen the ball on the top shelf before?" "Who played with it?" "What other toy is on the top shelf?" "What is Dick carrying?" Other relationships among characters may be brought out with such questions as "Is Dick taller than Jane?" "Is Jane taller than Sally?" "Who is tallest, Dick, Jane, or Sally?" "Who is shortest?" Discussion can then demonstrate the relationship between the height of the character and the relative position of the shelves. The teacher may say, for example, "Sally is the shortest. Which shelf will she use?" "Dick is the tallest. Which shelf will be his?"

On the following day the children turn to the next page of the reading-readiness text to demonstrate to the teacher and to themselves how well they have been able to use associations and relationships in recalling which toys should be placed where on the shelves.

As children try to remember where the toys belong, they will need to recall the logic of the associations. Dick, the tallest, uses the top shelf. The toys that Dick plays with are the ball, the mitt, and the airplane. Sally, the shortest, uses the bottom shelf, and her toys are the rabbit, the umbrella, and Tim. And so, as the children mark the page they learn for themselves that it is easy to remember an arrangement when they think about how different objects and groups of objects are related to one another.

To strengthen the ability to make associations and to help children form visual images for the purpose of remembering, the teacher can use one or more of the following activities.

Arrange on a table such things as a knife, fork, paintbrush, jacks, a rubber ball, and paintbox. Direct the children to look at each object, decide which are used together, and try to form mental pictures of these pairs. Then cover the objects and ask children to try to name them in pairs.

The pictures of pies, cakes, fruits, meats, and vegetables accumulated for playing the "Restaurant" game (p. 127) may be used in a new game, "Going to the Store." The teacher says, "Billy's mother sent him to the store to buy these things." She then shows the class the pictures of a group of items. When children have had an opportunity to study the pictures, she asks, "How do you think Billy will be able to remember everything he is supposed to get?" Depending on the items the teacher has shown, children should be able to identify certain relationships. Lettuce, for example, goes with tomatoes for a salad; milk is good to drink with cookies; bacon goes with eggs for breakfast.

This type of experience can then be followed by a page of pictures on which children identify those items that "go together," such as the following.

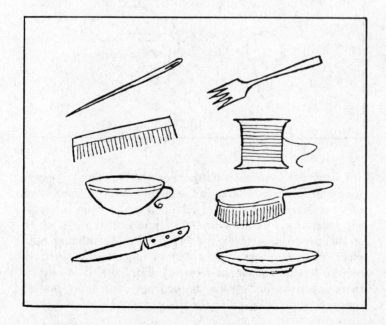

Part-whole relationships also can be used as clues for remembering. The teacher may use a set of pictures such as the following, saying as she shows them, "Each picture on the left side shows something that is a part of one of the things pictured on the right." Allow children time to identify the part-whole pairs and then ask who can remember the pairs without looking again at the picture.

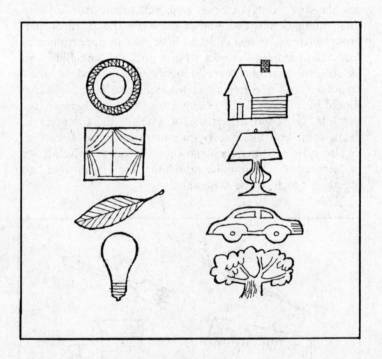

Classifying is another aid to remembering. Outlining, for example, is a traditional and valuable way to remember content, since ideas that are classified under main headings are more easily remembered than unclassified ideas. Even at the pre-reading level, the beginnings of outlining take place when children classify certain objects in a story or picture for the purpose of remembering. Suppose in a story there is a passage: "Mother needed hot dogs, buns, butter, mustard, and potato chips for the picnic. She asked Bobby to go to the store for her." If a child mentally classifies these items as *things to eat at a picnic,* he will find it easier than otherwise to remember the items. He will not be likely to include such things as turnips and pot roast when he tries to retell the story.

An exercise such as the following is helpful in promoting the ability to classify and remember items. Say, "Draw a line from each little picture to the kind of store in which you could buy that thing. Then say the names of the things you marked for each store. After you are through, put your paper away and see how many of the items you can remember."

In classifying the items by associating them with the store where they may be bought, the child reduces the eight items to two groups of four, each group associated with a concrete memory cue, namely, *toy store* or *market.*

Another scheme for remembering is a *chaining of ideas.* If each idea can be linked to another idea, as in a chain, then recalling the first idea will automatically set off the chain of associated ideas. Attempting to create images of what may have happened between two events will help children to develop this feeling of the relatedness of events. Present two pictures such as the following.

Say to the class: "The first picture shows the first part of a story. The last picture shows what happened last. Can you make a picture in your mind of what should be placed in the middle? What do you think happened between the first and last pictures?"

All the above exercises strengthen and develop a child's abilities for the purpose of remembering. With the techniques he learns through participation in these exercises he should find it progressively easier to observe details carefully, to associate ideas, to see relationships between objects and between concepts, to create visual and auditory images, and to associate images and ideas in sequence.

Reacting to ideas

As children learn to share the experiences of their storybook friends, they live more and more vividly in the stories. They chuckle with amusement at the antics of the characters and sigh with relief when a predicament is solved. The stories become a part of their own experiences, too, as the children identify themselves with a character and feel that what happens to that character also happens to themselves It is time, when children have reached this level of interpretation, to ask evaluative questions that will provoke thoughtful reactions to the storybook characters and their activities.

"What would *you* have done if you had been _____? Can you think of a better way for _____ to have acted when _____? Do you think this story is a true story or a fairy story?" These and other questions help children to evaluate, to decide what the story means to them privately.

A child may enjoy sharing the experiences of a storybook prince or princess for a while, but he should also recognize his own personality apart from the story. He should be able to step out of the story and relate the experiences to himself. The boy who says, "I like that story because I'd like to be a cowboy," or "I like that story because I'd like to be a ranger," recognizes the difference between fantasy and fact, and recognizes his wish to model his behavior after that of one of his heroes. On the other hand, he may not wish to be exactly like the hero. He may prefer to have had the story turn out differently. He may think a certain part of the action is not plausible; or he may object to the behavior of one of the characters.

At the pre-reading level teachers should help children to react to pictures and picture-stories with reference to themselves and to real life situations. While they are looking at a picture of a toy store, for example, the children guess not only which toy the boy in the picture is going to choose, but also which toy they would want if they were selecting one for themselves. They should make judgments as to whether the picture-boy chose wisely or not, and decide what they would do with the toy if they had it. By relating the picture-story to life situations, evaluating the action as a right or wrong thing for a character to do, or deciding what they themselves would do in such a case, children develop a healthy attitude towards ideas, probing their merit and accepting or rejecting them on the basis of sound evaluation.

THE OUTCOME OF INTERPRETATION

The outcome of evaluative interpretation is the integration of new ideas with the total personality. Some ideas are merely added to other ideas to increase knowledge; others may bring about the modification and reorganization of previously held ideas. For example, if a child who has learned to fear cats becomes acquainted, through a picture or story, with a friendly, playful kitten, he may compare this experience with his previous experiences with cats and conclude, "Not all cats are mean; kittens won't hurt you."

Gradually this child may develop a more tolerant and less emotional reaction to cats.

Thus a child's experience with the stories and activities of the pre-reading program may modify old patterns of thinking and serve as a basis not only for future action but also for future interpretation of pictures and later of printed language. Each interpretation, carefully and thoughtfully assimilated, provides just that much more experience upon which to base the next interpretation and the next evaluation.

BIBLIOGRAPHY

Arbuthnot, May Hill. *Children and Books*, Revised. Chicago: Scott, Foresman and Company, 1957. Background information about children's literature that should be available to every language arts teacher. Discusses origins of various types of children's literature and provides suggestions for using each type in various teaching situations. Includes a fifty-three page bibliography of literary materials for children.

————. *Poetry Time*. Chicago: Scott, Foresman and Company, 1951. May Hill Arbuthnot reading selections from *Time for Poetry*. Includes suggestions for participation. Album of three records, 78 r.p.m. Recorded by RCA Victor for Scott, Foresman.

————. *Time for Poetry*, School Edition, Revised. Chicago: Scott, Foresman and Company, 1959. A representative collection of poetry for children. Poems are organized by subject matter. Included are poems about people, poems about animals, poems about travel, poems about play, humorous and nonsense verse, verses of magic and make-believe, poems about the weather, the seasons, and the holidays, and poems of wisdom and beauty.

Gray, William S. *On Their Own in Reading*, Revised. Chicago: Scott, Foresman and Company, 1960. For the teacher who is looking for a thorough explanation of the word perception process. Includes chapters on the role of word perception in reading, the various stages of word analysis, and the use of the dictionary as an aid to word perception.

Robinson, Helen M.; Monroe, Marion; and Artley, A. Sterl. *We Read Pictures*. With W. Cabell Greet, Linguistic Advisor. Chicago: Scott, Foresman and Company, 1962. A pre-reading text that introduces children to essential disciplines and some of the basic skills and attitudes needed for early success in reading.

chapter seven

The Causes of Difficulties in Learning to Read

Even with the teacher's best efforts to develop all of the skills basic to learning to read, some boys and girls will not acquire the needed levels of maturity as rapidly as will others. Each child will progress only as rapidly as his natural endowments plus his linguistic experiences permit. Some children may be further hindered from reaching the maturity needed for beginning reading by any of a variety of special handicaps. These handicaps may be physical, such as a hearing loss; they may be social, such as inadequate experience with oral language of the right kind; or they may be psychological or emotional, such as lack of self-confidence.

Severe problems in some of these areas may require assistance from a specialist. However, it helps many boys and girls a great deal simply to know that they have the sympathy and understanding of the classroom teacher. Recognizing the nature of the difficulty often relieves much of the tension that has surrounded the problem and leads to simple remedies that lie well within the province of the classroom teacher.

If the school provides referral services for specially handicapped children, the teacher will naturally make use of these services. In other instances she may alert parents to the nature of the difficulty and, if the problem is serious enough, encourage them to seek medical assistance from their family physician.

But most of all the teacher needs to be sensitive to the possible existence of certain specific difficulties with which pupils may be trying to cope. Once she knows the danger signals and knows how to interpret them, she is prepared to give her pupils the maximum help possible within the classroom situation.

This chapter has been designed to help teachers to spot the danger signals for the following kinds of problems: emotional maladjustments, problems resulting from changed hand preference, visual defects, hearing defects, neurological defects, illness in general, mental retardation, and social and linguistic deprivation.

EMOTIONAL PROBLEMS

A child's emotional balance or imbalance has an effect upon his ability to learn and to retain what he has learned. Emotionally disturbed children who are placed in reading situations where they are under pressure to learn but whose attitudes are not ready for learning may embroil reading into their general emotional disturbance. Anxieties, hostilities, withdrawals, and other psychological blocks that are often difficult to overcome may be set up with reference to reading.

A little boy of nearly six sat on the steps of his front porch early in the morning of the first day of school. From there he could see the school only a block away. Proudly dressed in his new clothes, with unusually clean ears and hands, he eagerly awaited the time to leave. When at last the school bell rang, he jumped from the steps—but instead of running toward the school as he had planned, he fled in panic into the house and buried his face against his mother's apron.

"Why, what's the matter, son?" she questioned. "I thought you wanted to go to school."

"I do—I do—but I don't know how that teacher looks!" he wailed.

So do the bravest of us often flee back to the familiar when the time comes to go on to the unknown.

Almost every child, even the best adjusted, has at least a few momentary anxieties as he enters a new classroom. "I just thought I'd bring my teddy to school," one youngster said anxiously the first day as he clutched the well-worn toy. The presence of his beloved friend helped this boy to feel more at home in the new surroundings.

Making the classroom a friendly place

The physical appearance of the classroom has an important bearing upon the child's ability to make a happy transition from home to school. Informal, homelike arrangements of desks, tables, and chairs are more inviting than a formal and somewhat forbidding row-by-row arrangement of screwed-down desks. If a first-grade teacher inherits a formal room that cannot be changed, she can at least soften its looks with pictures, plants, and cozy corners. Yet, important as the physical appearance of a room is in attracting children, the emotional climate is even more important. This climate can best be illustrated by instances in which it has been achieved.

"Oh, Mother," said one boy, rushing in from his first day at school, "there's a little drawer in my table just for me, and the teacher put some crayons in it, and some paper, and a card with *my* name on it. And tomorrow I'm going to sit there and color." A sense of belonging had been established in this child by giving him a place for his equipment and a personal name card.

"I've got to be there tomorrow because I'm going to count the boys," another child said. He wanted to return to do what he felt was "his job," a task that was really necessary. His teacher in her skillful way had made every child feel that he had an important contribution to make to the group.

The comments made by these children illustrate little ways in which teachers have built up a happy climate in which the children feel a sense of "belonging," of "being needed," and of having a relationship of friendship with the teacher.

The five-year-old level of emotional growth is usually one of comparative calm once the child is adjusted to going to school. At this age, children like to practice the things they can do well, and thus they develop the emotional security and self-confidence that will lead them to the six-year-old level of boisterous aggressiveness, overestimation of abilities, competitiveness, and desire to dominate. The five-year-old often seems more poised and adept than the six-year-old, but the reason is that he does not try such difficult things and consequently has more success in what he attempts. His greater placidity is caused by immaturity rather than by control. He needs his mother or a mother-substitute to be near at hand, and in school he needs to feel that his teacher is the "class mother" who will arrange for his care and comfort and let him help with little services.

Five-year-olds feel more secure in classrooms where there is a simple, repetitive routine. It helps them to know what is coming next, where to find and put away materials, what they are expected to do and how to do it. Within the framework of a well-structured routine, they need periods of freedom to run about and talk, play noisily, and enjoy large-muscle activities. Freedom without structure or routine creates anxiety, because the child does not know the limitations of the environment and cannot see the goal of his activity.

Developing self-confidence

Children who are at the five-year-old level of emotional development (whether they are actually five or older) lack the enterprise for such a prolonged and demanding activity as learning to read. Some may be avid for stories and picture books and would like to learn to read if they could magically acquire the skill. However, when put to the task of making the careful discriminations and forming the associations required in accurate word recognition, they usually find the effort too difficult and tend to reject further work in reading. Just as a bad fall when taking his first steps may retard an infant's further efforts to walk alone, so exposing a child to reading before he achieves enough emotional maturity to succeed is likely to give him a serious setback in his desire to learn. Teachers should learn to think in terms of the emotional level of the child rather than his actual age, for some children at six and seven may still be at the five-year-old level of emotional maturity. The following case illustrates the possible bad effects of pressuring a child to try to read before he is emotionally ready to learn.

Because Billy would not yet be six years old in September, a decision had to be made about whether he should begin first grade. The school he was to attend had only annual promotions, so he could either enter at five and a half, as the youngest child in the class, or wait a year until he would be six and a half and one of the older children in the class. Because Billy was large for his age and because his parents were naturally ambitious for him, he was entered as the youngest child. Unfortunately, however, his emotional growth was not so accelerated as his height and weight. While he was as big as the six-year-olds, he was overwhelmed by their greater enterprise and aggressiveness. They soon outstripped him in reading, to the disappointment of his parents and to his own chagrin. He said plaintively, "Reading's too hard for me," and he put forth no effort but dreamed away the time spent in the reading circle.

The following year he was entered again in the first grade, but the zest for learning to read was gone. The books and stories were "old stuff" to him. He had heard the plots and knew what would happen next. It is far easier to teach a child for the first time than to revise unfortunate attitudes and establish new ones. Billy did learn to read and, in time, became the good reader he had the natural aptitude for being. But it took special understanding and skillful handling by both teacher and parents to undo the harm resulting from a premature and unsuccessful beginning.

By six years of age, most children have developed enough self-confidence to want to conquer new fields. They want to explore the limits of their abilities and are in the mood for adventuresome activities, both physical and mental. They believe in themselves enough to try anything, and they can put this trait to good use in approaching reading. But although children at this stage are enthusiastic "starters," they have not yet acquired the emotional stability for prolonged effort; hence, lessons should be brief and table assignments short enough so that they can be completed before fatigue sets in. Then, when the habit of finishing work becomes established, the teacher may gradually lengthen the tasks, help the child keep the habit of finishing, and enable him to grow in his ability to work for longer and longer periods.

Six-year-olds make many mistakes and do not mind doing so if they are not scolded or shamed. Making mistakes is a part of their enthusiastic, impulsive type of learning—and, indeed, is one way of learning. By seven, however, many children have become very sensitive to mistakes and are unduly cautious. Some of this sensitivity to error comes through social training, in classrooms where teachers strive too hard for perfection. When six-year-olds make a mistake, the teacher should call it "a good try" or remark, "You're getting closer now," thinking of the mistake not as reprehensible but as a good attempt in the right direction. A "guess" is based on some kind of data, even if the child cannot explain it; it is a judgment made on the basis of past experience. To say "Do not guess" is almost the same as to say "Do not think." Remember, too, that the child receives praise when he guesses correctly, and it is assumed that he *knows* the right answer. Actually, of course, he may not have known any more than when he guessed wrong—he just was more fortunate or, for some reason, got on the right track and used better judgment. Fear of making mistakes has crippled many a child's ability to learn, dampened his ardor for working, robbed him of self-confidence, and placed an emotional block between his potential capacities and their free development.

Releasing emotional tensions

At any stage of growth there are individuals who for various reasons get out of step with the normal trends of development. Occasionally, a bright child will fail to exhibit a desire to read or may even show a desire *not* to read, just as at an earlier age he may not want to eat properly, may refuse to be toilet-trained, may delay talking, or may fail to adjust socially. For some reason emotional tensions have developed about certain areas of the child's development and have blocked or inhibited normal growth, perhaps even turning the line of growth backwards into regression or away from normal goals into negativism.

Two six-year-old children from the same first grade came into the office of a special-reading teacher. Shirley went at once to the bookshelf, where she found several little books that she had seen before. As she picked up each familiar friend she made pleasant sounds of greeting.

"We have this book at home," she smiled. "Isn't the baby's picture cute? I can hardly wait until I know how to read these stories all by myself."

Gordon did not even glance at the books. He went at once to the toy shelf, where he selected a gun equipped with a number of rubber-tipped suction darts. Fitting darts into the gun, he shot at the target, smiling with delight at any good "hit." Then, spying an attractive primary reader propped up on the book rack, he scowled.

"Oh, you've got one of those books, too. Well, I just hate that old book." Taking careful aim, he fired, and soon the book was covered with darts.

Shirley's experiences with books had been happy ones. She was stable and emotionally poised, and she was "all set" for learning to read. Gordon's experiences were quite different. He was repeating the first grade because he had learned not even a word the year before. Anxious parents and a baffled teacher had tried to help him, and much of the work had centered around the hapless little book which he had just used as a target. His associations with this book were anything but pleasant ones—staying after school while the other children were playing outdoors, and doing homework with parents who now scolded, now pleaded, now punished, now wept, and who continually compared him with a brilliant older sister, the family pride and joy.

Gordon's mother, in discussing his reading problem, said, "Reading isn't the only thing he won't do. He is negative to everything. He just doesn't seem to be at all like the rest of us. Bringing him up has been one constant battle, almost from his birth."

Shirley and Gordon are both intelligent children with entirely different attitudes toward reading. Shirley is ready emotionally for reading, but Gordon's attitudes toward reading reflect his unhappy experiences. He has defeated all efforts to teach him to read, just as he has held out in other ways against conforming to the demands of an environment in which he feels rejected, unwanted, "different," and fundamentally insecure—an environment in which he feels he must battle for his very right to be himself. His unfavorable attitudes toward reading are only one aspect of a deep-seated emotional and personality disturbance. Fortunately, there are many Shirleys in every classroom and only a few Gordons, but before a teacher can help one of the Gordons, she must understand and accept his feelings and work with him toward a new orientation to himself and to reading.

Preventing emotional upsets

Little children rarely can talk spontaneously about their feelings, but often in their free-play activities they will dramatize situations that give the teacher insight into their problems. A dollhouse can be placed in one corner of the classroom, equipped with mother, father, brother, sister, and baby dolls, and with living room, kitchen, bedroom, and bath. Perhaps there can even be a toy schoolroom nearby, with a teacher doll and pupil dolls. As the teacher observes a child's play with the dolls, she may notice how he expresses feelings toward a parent or sibling or toward teacher or classmates by pretending acts of violence, by imitating normal home or school activities, or by creating emotionally colored episodes.

The teacher should accept without criticism the child's free play and his right to his own feelings, for it enables him to obtain a real release of his emotions. For example, if a child pushes the baby doll off the roof, he may "work off" in play a resentment against being displaced by a new arrival. If he thereafter puts the baby doll to bed to get well, he may be expressing a protective feeling which he also has. Dramatizations of episodes in the classroom can be very revealing indeed to the teacher who has the courage to look and the objectivity to understand. Through play, the child reflects his relationship to the people and events in his environment, and he may gradually shift from destructive to constructive dramatizations. He must, however, feel secure enough in his relationship with the teacher to be able to display and talk about his feelings in front of her. If she accepts him, he may use the playhouse for emotional growth by releasing his feelings and tensions, and he may gradually clarify the reasons for his feelings and thus gain insight.

A nook or corner of the room partially screened from the rest of the class and equipped with a small rocking chair and other child-sized furniture and toys is also very helpful. When a child who has difficulty in adjusting to a large group of children grows tense and verges on tears, he may withdraw into the quiet of the playroom, where he can play alone while he recovers his emotional poise. Or he may like to play there with one other child. Adjusting to one child at a time may be a large enough problem for him, but as he learns to play successfully with now this child and now another one, he will grow in ability to adjust to a small learning group of six or eight children. Later, his sense of security will be developed enough so that he can work with the whole group.

Many emotional upsets may be prevented if a teacher is sensitive to a child's tensions and helps him to find ways of releasing them before an explosion takes place. Permitting an outlet for expressing hostilities in a legitimate way by dramatization (such as by playing the big bad wolf) helps disperse the feelings. Permitting the child to regress for a while to a younger level of play and to easier materials may also give him a welcome respite. Emotional maturity is acquired gradually—and even adults cannot always maintain a high level of behavior under emotional stress. In times of intense emotional strain, it is comforting to turn to routine or manual activities, for temporarily one is incapable of work requiring high intellectual and creative abilities. Periods of growth and regression and then further growth are typical of all learning curves.

Drawing, finger painting, painting, and modeling are all good outlets for tension, and an observer trained in the psychology of children's artistic expressions may find valuable leads to understanding personality. The restricted child may fill only a tight little corner of a paper with rigid, closed-in figures. An aggressive child may make a figure which he pounds down, if in clay; scrubs over, if in paint or crayon; or maltreats as an effigy.

Music also has its power to soothe or excite. "Do-what-the-music-tells-you" is a good outlet for bodily activity to express emotions. Marching, skipping, and singing games may tempt even the most withdrawn child to participate. And after a period of musical skipping, two children on the verge of battle may forget their difficulties and settle down into peaceful cooperation.

Stories and poems give vicarious experiences in which the child relives emotionally the feelings of the characters. Literature, which is verbal expression, is especially helpful. Not only does the child feel deeply the experiences of the characters, but he hears emotionally toned ideas expressed beautifully in language. He may gradually develop ability to verbalize his own feelings and in verbal discussion may obtain a greater intellectual clarification of his problems than is possible through any other means.

Reading ability and the total personality pattern

Just as teachers adjust to the physical and mental characteristics of young children, so they should also understand methods of helping children grow in personality. Since personality difficulties so frequently spring from early experiences in the home, parent-teacher conferences are important in learning why children behave as they do.

A teacher should remember, in interviewing parents, that mothers and fathers have feelings too, and unless they trust her wisdom and integrity they will not confide in a teacher some of the things that might help her most in understanding the child. Confidential information about a child and his home imposes an obligation on the teacher to be worthy of the trust and to use the information wisely and for the benefit of the child. If a teacher feels that she is not able to meet this responsibility, or if the case is a baffling one, she should refer the child and his parents to a child-guidance or mental-hygiene clinic for help. She can then cooperate with the psychiatrist, psychologist, and psychiatric social worker in the case, obtaining help from them, in turn, in her efforts to meet the child's problem.

The following cases from a reading clinic illustrate how emotional disturbances in the child's growth may hinder his progress in reading by rendering him unable to respond normally to reading instruction. These two cases have been selected to show the role of the first-grade teacher in the development of emotional readiness for reading.

Charles was a dreamy-eyed little boy of seven who came to the reading clinic because he had made very little progress in learning to read, although he had above-average intelligence and was ready to read according to several reading-readiness tests.

When Charles was fourteen months old, a baby sister was born, and the routines of his life were suddenly disrupted. In the first place, his mother disappeared for a long, long time—ten days is almost forever to a toddler. When she returned she had with her a little infant on whom she lavished the attention and cuddling affection which Charles had missed so keenly during her absence. Charles, who was just beginning to say a few words and to acquire some rudimentary feeding and toilet habits, suddenly began to behave again as a younger infant. He demanded a bottle again, stopped talking, and in every way he could imitated the behavior of the new arrival. But instead of winning affection and cuddling, as the infant did, he received disapproval, irritated expressions, and scoldings. No longer a happy dumpling of a toddler, he began to lose weight and to fret and whine.

"I realized then we were making a mistake," said his mother, "and we should have prepared him in some way for the baby—but how can you prepare a little guy that isn't even talking yet? We tried to make it up to him when we saw how nervous he was getting, so after I'd fed the baby, I'd just take him onto my lap, and give him a bottle too. I began to treat them just alike, but that was a mistake, because then he didn't try to make any effort to be his own age."

To condense a long story, Charles began again to talk when precocious little Cathy began talking, and from then on he followed her lead. She was the first to stay dry, to pedal a tricycle, to make advances to playmates. Their positions were reversed as she outstripped him in poise and in emotional maturity. He continued to cling to his mother and to avoid new situations long after Cathy was out exploring the neighborhood on her own.

When it came time to go to school, however, he of course reached the age of entrance first.

"I had two of them crying that first day of school," said the mother, "Charles, who didn't want to go, and Cathy, who did."

Charles gradually adjusted to school, but most of the first grade he spent in "growing up" and learning to do things for himself.

"During the reading period, he would just smile and look at me trustingly with his big brown eyes," said his teacher. "When I would work with him alone, he would respond and learn a few words. I would stand by his desk and point to his place in the workbook, encouraging him to do the next item, and he would mark it. Then he would just sit patiently without touching the book until I came around again. The 'self-starter' was left out of his little motor, I guess. But he is getting better every day."

At the end of the first grade, he was still considerably behind the others in reading, and the problem of grade placement was uppermost in the minds of teacher, parents, and principal.

"He is beginning to adjust well now and to do things by himself," said the teacher. "I'd like to have him another year. I believe he will get along better next year. He is really ready now."

"You have done so much for Charles and for me, too, in understanding him, that I'd surely like to have you continue with him," said his mother. "But what will happen when Cathy is in the same room next year? I wish they would not have to be together, because he has been so much more independent since he has been separated from her. I, too, have learned more how to treat him as an older child, to give him the security he needs and yet make him feel proud of the things he is doing that she is not yet old enough to do. I am afraid he will lose what he has gained if she catches up with him."

"Our school is a small one and we have no half-term promotion and only one first grade," said the principal. "But our second-grade teacher is an understanding person, and she can take him from just where he is and let him continue to grow in the ways he needs to grow. He has accomplished much more than one year's growth in one year, even if his growth has been in emotional maturity rather than in academic achievement, and he needs the official stamp of approval by 'passing.' Perhaps next year he will take a spurt toward reading, now that he has acquired emotional readiness."

Charles' case was a relatively simple one to solve. His problems were met with understanding both at home and in the classroom situation, with conferences between teacher, parent, principal, and reading clinician. By the mid-term of the second grade, he was working with normal independence and was becoming slightly more aggressive. His reading achievement reflected the gains in emotional growth. He had no real difficulty in word perception and, once he had the self-reliance to apply himself, he was well on the road to catching up with his classmates. Compare the problems of Charles with those of Tony, given below.

Tony was born at a very inopportune time for his mother. Just when she had decided she could no longer bear an unhappy marriage with an erratic and quarrelsome husband, and when she was trying to make plans whereby she could take the two older children with her and set up a little business of her own, she discovered that Tony was on the way. To make matters worse, her entire pregnancy was one of illness and discomfort. Submissive and dependent by nature and fearful of a scene, she had not told her husband of her plans to leave him, and now with another child coming it seemed to her that the doorway to an independent life was permanently closed. Although her life seemed bleak, her husband did provide for her and the children in a feast-or-fast fashion, and by careful managing she had always saved a few extra dollars during good times to help in hard times.

"While waiting for Tony to come," she said, "I used to think of doing away with myself, and the baby with me. I thought bitterly that I was disillusioned and had no love left to give to anyone, even to a little innocent child who had no blame of his own. And when the baby was put in my arms I had no feeling for him. Those were wicked thoughts and I should not even say them—so I tried to make it up to the poor little babe, and did more for him than I ever did for the other two, who came when I was younger and had hope. Do you think a mother can mark a child by her thoughts? I mean, in his spirit? Because he never developed any feeling for anyone. He wants things only for himself. I am nothing to him. His father and sisters are nothing. School is nothing. Only for play he lives, and such play! Fires, and breaking up expensive toys, and showing off, and bragging."

Tony, the subject of his mother's discussion, proved to be a curly-headed, cherubic-looking boy of nearly six. With an I.Q. of 125 to give him ideas and with "no feeling for anyone," he was indeed the terror of the first grade. Quick to take part in the class when it appealed to him, he waited

for no one but "answered" out of turn all the teacher's
questions whether he knew the answers or not. He grabbed
the papers to pass them and buffeted his way to the head
of the line in passing to recess. On the days he did not care
to participate in the class activities, he stalked around the
room glowering, refused to obey requests, and was a law
unto himself. Reading had no appeal, and he never entered
into the reading classes except to disturb others. He loved
art work, however, and the classroom was most peaceful
when Tony was sitting at a table alone covering huge sheets
of paper with brilliantly colored bombers, battleships, and
burning buildings.

Tony's case needed to be approached from many angles.
His mother and father were referred to a psychiatrist, and
in talking out their problems with the doctor they achieved
a better understanding of their marriage. The mother
learned to see that her feelings of rejecting the child and
her guilt over such feelings were related to her inconsistent
treatment of the child—her overindulgence of him but her
failure to provide the real warmth he needed. She became
more accepting of Tony as she grew more accepting of
his father, and she was able to establish better routines for
the whole family at home. As she gave Tony more of her
real self, she was able to ask and receive more from him.
She no longer needed to indulge him with an excess of toys
and gifts as peace offerings to her conscience.

Paralleling the treatment of the parents, the reading clinic
studied Tony to see if he could learn to read. Since he was
so bright, it was hoped that actual achievement would bring
him self-respect and ability to gain recognition in legitimate
channels. A puppy that he admired was given to him, and
the snuggly, dependent little creature won from him real
protection and friendship and served as a basis for many
stories which he related to the teacher and which were
typed into "his own book." One of his drawings of a burning building was so brilliantly colored and really beautiful
artistically that it was chosen for a school poster for a fire-
prevention drive. Tony proudly thought of and copied an
appropriate caption under the picture. In the playroom at
clinic and school his activities gradually shifted from de-

structive types of play to more constructive activities. By the end of the year, he enthusiastically accepted reading and made real progress.

Tony's case was an involved one that required the combined approach of specialists in a number of fields to bring about improvement. The first-grade teacher learned to understand and accept him with kindliness and tolerance, even though he often threw her class into disorder and upset her plans. While accepting him (and she really liked her little tornado), she watched for any legitimate use of his abilities (the school poster for fire prevention) and gave him opportunities for the expression of constructive as well as destructive feelings (procuring for him the puppy he admired). She put no pressure on him to read, for fear of embroiling reading into his other hostilities, but she typed his little stories about the pup into a book "by Tony" for the good readers to read at the library table. Thus he gained respect as an "author" even before he became a "reader," and he developed a consuming desire to read his own book.

This bright and talented little boy very slowly, but steadily, found a place for himself at home and at school. Each legitimate success gave him more self-respect and developed his ability to respect others, too. He no longer needed to gain attention in antisocial ways, for he was readily accepted when he could enter games without disturbance.

The two cases of Charles and Tony, though different in type, illustrate the important contribution that teachers can make in working with the emotionally disturbed child. They illustrate also how a child's ability to learn to read is related to his total personality pattern and how, without an understanding of the child's basic emotional needs, the teacher is greatly handicapped in her attempts to teach him to read. For seriously disturbed children, first grade may well be spent in developing emotional readiness for reading rather than in placing emphasis on actual reading. To force reading on the emotionally disturbed youngster may merely involve reading in the child's total disturbance and thus make him hostile toward acquiring a necessary and important skill.

PROBLEMS RESULTING FROM CHANGED HAND PREFERENCE

Serious reading problems may develop if a child who naturally prefers his left hand has been pressured into using his right hand instead. His whole system of motor coordination may be affected, as well as his perception of space. The three following examples of the effects of changing handedness may illustrate the kinds of problems which are likely to develop.

Barbara, whose handedness was changed when she was six, became so confused that for several months she could not tell left from right, wrote mirror writing, and as often as not tried to read from right to left rather than from left to right.

Paul, whose teacher insisted that he use his right hand, did very little work while she was looking in his direction. The moment her back was turned, he quickly finished as much of his workbook as he could with his preferred left hand, but he was always ready to shift the pencil back to the right hand in case she looked around. By deception, he defeated his teacher's attempts to change his handedness, but his personality suffered from his guilty feelings in so doing.

A college student requested the help of a psychologist to speed up his writing. "I simply can't write fast enough to take exams," he said. "The minute I try to speed up, my writing becomes such a scrawl that neither I nor anyone else can read it." This student had been shifted from left- to right-handedness at the age of six. He learned to write with the right hand, but his writing consisted of a process of slow "drawing" of words. As an adult, he could develop no speed with the right hand. His preferred left hand had lost its natural facility through long disuse, so that he was as slow and awkward with it as he was in using his right hand. Shifting handedness had created a real problem for this student.

VISUAL DEFECTS

Visual defects of various kinds may retard learning to read. One worried six-year-old reported, after a few weeks in the first grade: "Mother, you'd better get some books and let me practice reading at home, because today I was the third dumbest one. If we don't get busy I might get to be the dumbest one."

An investigation of his problem revealed that he had a marked degree of myopia, or near-sightedness. From his position in the back of the room, he could not distinguish the words on the charts and chalkboard at the front, and naturally he could not read them. Children usually are not aware of their visual defects, since they believe everyone sees just as they do. Thus this conscientious pupil had decided that he must be "dumb" when he failed to read the words as the others did. Correcting his vision, moving his seat nearer to the chalkboard, and rapidly reviewing the words he had missed during the period when he could not see enabled this intelligent child to catch up with his group and to keep up thereafter.

It sometimes happens that even a very severe visual defect may be overlooked. One little girl had almost finished and failed first grade before either her teacher or her parents recognized that the child was growing blind. She bumped into children and objects and was scolded for being clumsy, but no one thought to question whether or not she could see the objects. Her peculiar responses to pictures in her book won her a reputation of being both "dumb" and "smart-alecky." One can imagine what a year of torment she went through before her visual defect was discovered. Now, after receiving adequate medical attention and being placed in a school for the blind, she is a happy, well-adjusted child. Intelligence tests designed for blind children have revealed that she is exceptionally bright.

Detecting visual defects

It is a common-sense procedure to have visual examinations for all children soon after they enter school. It is especially important to use the kind of visual screening test that will reveal the defects which may be handicaps in learning to read. Reliance on an inadequate vision test may be more damaging than using no test at all. The Snellen Test, which has been widely used and is still in use in some schools, is not adequate as a test of vision for school children since it identifies only the near-sighted child. The four visual screening tests listed below will aid the examiner in finding children who have several other types of visual defects.

Keystone Visual Survey Test (Betts Telebinocular)
Keystone View Co., Meadville, Pennsylvania.

Massachusetts Vision Test
Welch-Allyn Co., Skaneateles Falls, New York

Eames Eye Test
Harcourt, Brace and World, Inc., Tarrytown, New York

Ortho-Rater Tests of Visual Efficiency
Bausch & Lomb, Inc., Rochester 2, New York

These four tests may all be administered by a person without technical background if he is careful about following directions. They are not diagnostic tests but simply screening tests to give the teacher information as to which children need to be referred to a vision specialist. They are scored only *pass* or *fail*.[1]

Symptoms of eye difficulties which may be easily observed by the teacher include the following:

1. Unusual positions of holding book or head.

2. Narrowing the shape of the eye while looking at the chalkboard. (Near-sighted children try to shorten their eyeballs by pressing the lids against the ball of the eye or pushing the outside corners of their eyes up.)

3. Frequent looking up from close work or glancing out

[1] For further information about these tests, including relative reliability, usability, and cost, see Helen M. Robinson, "Visual Screening Tests for Schools," *Elementary School Journal*, 54 (December 1953), 217-222.

of the window to rest eyes. (This is characteristic of the far-sighted child.)

4. Rubbing the eyes to brush away the blur.

5. Holding hand over one eye while looking.

6. Watering, red-rimmed eyes.

7. Comments that words or pictures "jump" on the page, that objects are doubled or blurred.

8. Inability to keep the place in the book.

Some children adapt to visual defects by straining to see (and possibly damaging vision further), by superior intelligence in interpreting blurred images, by unusual drive toward reading, and by favorable personality factors such as persistence in spite of discomfort. The fact that some children do learn to read in spite of rather serious visual defects may mean that, had the defects been corrected early, the children might have been even better readers; undoubtedly they would have been far more comfortable while reading. The diagnosis and correction of vision is a problem for the eye specialist, but the *discovery* of children who should be referred to an eye specialist is a service teachers can render by being alert to possible symptoms.

Among the visual defects that are most likely to affect a child's ability to learn to read are excessive far-sightedness (hyperopia), hyperopic astigmatism, binocular incoordination (failure of the two eyes to work properly together), restricted visual fields, and aniseikonia (unequal size images from the two eyes).

Helping the visually handicapped

Visually handicapped children can learn to discriminate and organize what they *are* able to see just as well as can normally sighted children. The teacher should adjust to their handicaps by understanding where their difficulties are likely to occur. Near-sighted children should be seated near chalkboards and charts on which pictures and forms are plainly drawn in large size. These children usually do well with books and table work. Far-sighted children, on the other hand, may fatigue quickly during near work, and small details may be seen as blurred. When they look out of the window or at their neighbors' work, it may not be inattentiveness or distractibility; their eyes may need the rest from the close work. Children who have fusion difficulties may need time to find their place and to make the visual adjustments necessary to clear away the double images, if possible. Astigmatism distorts the small details of printed letters and words.

Correction of a child's visual defects before he learns to read is highly desirable and may prevent some types of reading difficulties. Pending such correction, the teacher should see to it that handicapped youngsters are seated where their work is well lighted; details that cannot be seen in dim or shadowy light may be seen under good light. Duplicated materials that are blurred or hazy will aggravate the children's visual difficulties, as will drawing on chalkboards that have been erased and re-erased.

In dealing with children who have visual difficulties, keep in mind the fact that no one can see through another's eyes. Little children, therefore, rarely suspect that they have trouble in seeing. Be reassuring when a child makes an error in visual discrimination and try to find ways to help him see better. Make an enlarged drawing on the blackboard, if necessary. Let him hold in his own hands, for a few moments of inspection, a picture or object which is to be displayed on the chalk ledge for group discussion. Allow him to take his reading-readiness booklet over to the window for better lighting of some item which he does not see clearly when he is in the circle grouped around the teacher. Help him to attain as much success as possible with the vision he has.

HEARING DEFECTS

Many infectious illnesses to which children are prone may result in some hearing loss. As a result, ear troubles are frequent among five- and six-year-olds. Even though hearing may not be permanently damaged, children sometimes go through periods of temporary hearing loss just at a period when the learning tasks require hearing acuity. A teacher should be on the alert to discover children who are even temporarily hard of hearing and give them seats near enough to hear her voice. Symptoms of difficulties in hearing are:

1. Holding head to one side to favor the better ear.
2. Strained and tense expression while listening.
3. Inattentiveness and ignoring directions.
4. Lack of response when called upon.
5. Earache, running ears, and wax-filled canals.
6. Speech difficulties and confusion of words sounding nearly alike.
7. Withdrawn behavior and failure to participate with the group.

Detecting defects in hearing

Using the entire class as a standard, the teacher may detect the more obviously hard-of-hearing children by using a "ticking watch" or "whispered numbers" test. For the "ticking watch" test, slowly bring a watch (the same one must be used for all) closer and closer to the child's ears (each ear in turn) until he reports that he can hear the tick. Since the majority of children will respond when the watch reaches a certain easily determined distance, it is a simple matter to pick out the children who need to have the watch brought unusually close to their ears. For the "whispered numbers" test, make a list of about ten to fifteen numbers, such as 35, 66, 89, and so forth. Whisper these numbers while standing six feet behind each child and have him repeat the numbers aloud. Notice which children have unusual difficulty when compared to the rest of the class. These two tests are an informal way to find those who need a more intensive analysis.

Many children of this age develop an apparent deafness similar to real deafness, reflecting a preoccupation with thoughts and activities of their own. The seven-year-old is especially likely to develop this absent-minded "deafness" without a true hearing loss. Sometimes children who are overly nagged and scolded at home develop a protective "deafness." To differentiate between the truly hard of hearing and the apparently deaf, the teacher may need to call upon the school physician. Audiometer tests are helpful in diagnosing hearing loss, particularly losses of sensitivity to pitches in certain frequency ranges. Some children hear low tones but cannot hear high tones. Sometimes the pitch ranges of the human voice are affected, so that the child may hear the voice as if muffled, like a radio with the low tones turned up and the high tones cut down. It is especially distressing to hear a voice with tone qualities too blurred for comprehension. The following case illustrates the difficulty as well as the importance of diagnosing partial deafness.

Betty was a little girl who got along well in her reading-readiness workbooks as long as the pages dealt with visual discrimination of pictures, story interpretation, or reasoning. But she had great difficulty with the pages which required her to find pictures of objects that rhyme, or that begin with the same sound. Her teacher regarded her at first as simply "erratic" and prone to periods of inattention. As time went on, however, the teacher began to notice that her "inattention" usually occurred when someone was talking. Once she requested Betty to open the *door*, and when the child opened a *drawer* the teacher suspected deafness and asked that Betty be given an audiometer test.

"I'm not at all sure she is deaf," the teacher said. "Today she turned quickly toward the window when a little bird chirped very softly in a nearby tree. She also looked up when I dropped my purse, which made a soft thud. And when Mr. Brown, the principal, was in the room, she heard what he said, although he has a very low voice."

The audiogram confirmed the teacher's suspicion that Betty had a hearing defect and revealed the reason for the apparent inconsistencies in her behavior toward sounds. Betty's audiogram revealed normal hearing for high tones (such as a bird's chirp) and low tones (such as a soft thud), but there was a marked deficiency in hearing tones in the range of frequency of the human voice, especially the voices of women and children. She could hear men's voices, nearly an octave lower, more easily than women's voices. Betty's type of partial deafness was hard to recognize without special instruments, since she responded so normally to many tones. After the teacher knew what to expect, she was able to adapt to Betty's difficulty in the classroom and prevent the humiliation and bewilderment that come to a child who is accused of inattention when she actually is deaf. The teacher also gave special stress to the sound-discrimination exercises in the reading-readiness books in order to help Betty develop the best discrimination of which she was capable.

As with visual defects, so with hearing defects—the teacher may render a service to children and parents by discovering cases of possible hearing loss and making sure that they are referred to ear specialists. The first grade is an especially good time to conserve both vision and hearing before possible defects resulting form childhood illnesses become too serious and psychological complications arise.

Helping the child with hearing difficulties

The teacher should make allowances for the frequent hearing difficulties of this age, both physical and emotional. She should be generous in repeating directions and explanations for the benefit of children who have hearing difficulties. She should also arrange for frequent reviews and should briefly summarize each day what was done the day before, so that a child who missed by not "hearing" may have an opportunity to clarify points he did not understand.

The habit of asking a member of the class to repeat oral directions or explanations immediately after the teacher is a good one for first-grade teachers to cultivate. The teacher should bear in mind that children will not call out "Louder!" from the back of the room, as adults do in a meeting when they cannot hear the speaker. Children tend merely to take such portion of the directions as they do hear and make up the rest; or they give up trying to hear altogether and withdraw into their own daydreams. Screaming does not help children to hear, because as the lifted voice becomes higher it may reach the pitch levels that are often hardest to discriminate. Also, "deafness" of emotional origin may be a protection against just such screaming. A low, pleasant voice with clear enunciation and flexible (as contrasted

with monotonous) range is the teacher's goal. Such a voice
may catch the attention of those who habitually ignore
speech sounds and may give the child who has a true hearing
loss a better chance to read the lips and judge what is
being said. Above all, the hard-of-hearing child should
always be given a seat near the source of sound.

Many slight hearing defects are overlooked because the
children respond so normally to the usual classroom sounds.
Not until they are required to make some particularly
difficult discrimination between sounds do these children
reveal their difficulties. The following case illustrates the
serious effects that an undetected hearing difficulty can have
upon learning.

Bob was a boy of average intelligence, but when he
reached the eighth grade at the age of thirteen he was able
to read only at the fourth-grade level. Even then he found
it difficult to distinguish such pairs of words as *chatter,
shatter; ever, every; bought, brought.* Even when given a
first-grade book, he could not read with complete accuracy.
Patty became *Patsy, went* became *want,* and so on. In
speaking, Bob used such phrases as *in the distant* instead of
in the distance. He said, "I have trouble with my *vowels*
and *constants.*" One morning he spent twenty minutes of
a study period in searching a dictionary for the spelling
of the word *appreciate,* painstakingly going through page
after page, only to learn, frustrated and discouraged—the
dictionary still open to the P's—that he had not heard the
first syllable of the word. Bob's teacher called him careless.

An audiometer test revealed that Bob had a slight hearing
loss at the high-frequency ranges—enough to lower his
sensitivity to some of the higher frequency speech sounds,
but not enough to interfere with most of his normal classroom activities or to prevent successful remedial instruction
in reading. In Bob's case, auditory training in listening for
the various qualities of sounds, with exercises like those
described in Chapter 4 (stepped up to an interest level that
would appeal to an older boy), soon increased his ability
to discriminate sounds to such a marked degree that his
former confusions in speaking, reading, and spelling gradu-

ally disappeared. How fortunate it would have been for Bob if the hearing loss had been identified when he was five or six years old and the auditory training given at that time. Seven long years of failure, misunderstanding, and learning of faulty language patterns could have been largely avoided.

In all auditory training it is important to try to consider the feelings of the hard-of-hearing child. Never should he be placed in a position where he is made to feel inferior because of his handicap. With friendly help he may avoid developing the lonely, withdrawn personality that so often is the result of even a slight hearing loss.

NEUROLOGICAL DEFECTS

Neurological problems, since they are usually more difficult to identify than problems of vision or hearing, frequently go undiagnosed. They are perhaps more insidious, too, for the relationship of symptoms to causes is not fully understood and appropriate remedial methods have not been devised for all cases. A child must have an adequately organized central nervous system in order to coordinate and link visual symbols (printed language) with their meanings (auditory and oral language symbols). These associations take place in the central nervous system, where association fibers between the sense areas of the brain are coordinated with each other and with motor responses. If the brain has been damaged by birth injuries or by illness, so that the association fibers are injured, there may be an organic basis for a child's difficulty in learning to read. Defective intra-uterine development, birth injuries, acute infections and diseases (especially measles, whooping cough, and virus infections) in infancy, before speech has developed and while the nervous system is yet highly immature, may be responsible for a child's difficulty in forming correct reading associations.

Fortunately, the nervous system is flexible and other brain areas may take over to some extent the functions of damaged areas. Children with various neurological injuries may find ways to learn if teachers are experimental and provide many avenues of approach to each printed word.

A pleasant experience for all children that is also a useful test for neurological defects is the following. While a child keeps his eyes closed, the teacher traces with her finger lightly on the child's bare arm, or on the back of his hand, some simple symbol such as an X or O or square. The child is then asked to go to the board and draw as nearly as he can the symbol he thinks the teacher made on his arm. When children have learned the names of the symbols, they may respond simply by naming the symbol.

As a practice device for children who have difficulty with this exercise, the teacher may put several such symbols on the board, saying, "I will make one of these on your hand. Close your eyes and think carefully as you feel my finger on your hand and see if you can tell which one of these figures I make." This kind of practice may help children who have difficulty in responding to the kines-thetic stimulus.

Many children—more than teachers suspect—suffer from mild neurological injuries or illnesses that do not render the child conspicuously handicapped but nevertheless do retard learning. The following case illustrates a severe reading dis-ability of neurological origin in a bright, well-adjusted boy.

Tom, aged seven, was referred to the reading clinic for a check on his marked inability to remember words. So serious was his problem that his teacher suspected he must be "word-blind." Printed words had no meaning to Tom, although he remembered stories well and could repeat verbatim the text on many pages of his book. When an individual word was pointed out, Tom's friendly face grew troubled, and he could never identify the word.

"I ought to know the words," he said wistfully to the examiner at the reading clinic. "I know my book almost by heart. But that doesn't count. You've got to know what the printing is, not just what the story is."

Tom's social history was that of a normal boy who was loved and accepted by sensible parents who shared his feelings of bewilderment over his reading problem. His parents said, "Tom's a good boy. He wants to learn to read, and we'd gladly help him. But we aren't experts, and we don't want to confuse him. We need help in finding out what is best for Tom."

Tom's teacher said, "There isn't a boy in the room who tries harder, or who wants more sincerely to read, than Tom. That's one reason why I'd do anything—give any extra time or effort—to help him. But the usual methods just don't work in his case, even though he has a good I.Q."

Tom's physical examination revealed a healthy child with good vision and hearing, but his health history indicated that he had had two serious illnesses with complications at the age of twelve months. A severe case of measles was followed almost immediately by severe whooping cough. Tom was referred to a neurologist, who made an electro-encephalogram (a tracing of brain waves) which, in Tom's case, indicated pathology of the central nervous system that possibly had taken place as a complication of the two infections in infancy (while the nervous system was relatively immature) or might have been the result of an encephalitis which had never been recognized as such. The injury involved the association pathways of the brain in which visual patterns are linked with auditory patterns— hence Tom's very real difficulty in attaching language meaning to printed symbols, even though he could memorize the language patterns (stories) without effort.

Tom's parents and teacher were told of the organic basis of his difficulty and the need for special methods. Tracing large models of words with the finger while saying the name of the word aloud gave Tom an extra associational link that enabled him to learn to recognize words. He was able to form visual-kinesthetic associations and also kinesthetic-auditory association, and by this formula could by-pass the deficient visual-auditory association pathways. By special methods Tom's teacher was able to help him learn and thus to prevent the fine personality he had achieved from suffering the effects of failure and discouragement.

He remarked after a few months' training, "I'm not really good yet—maybe I'll never get to be *fast* at reading—but gosh! I thought I'd *never* get it. Say—listen to me read this page, will you? Cover up the picture—I don't need anything but the printing! Don't mind if I'm slow, now. Slow but sure—that's me." And slowly, but accurately and triumphantly, he read not only one but a dozen pages before he was willing to stop.

Tom's case emphasizes the need for thoroughgoing physical and neurological examinations for those children who do not learn to read even though eager to read and apparently ready to learn. Tom's only peculiarity in doing the exercises in the reading-readiness books had been a slight blocking—a hesitation, or fumbling for words, when asked to name a row of pictures—and a brief memory span for unrelated words or objects. Related words and events, as in storytelling, had been remembered without difficulty.

ABSENCE FROM SCHOOL

The five-, six-, and seven-year-old period is one of frequent illness and absence from school. It is unfortunate that the age when children begin to learn a skill as important to their future lives as reading should also be the age of frequently disrupted school attendance. Teachers need to adjust their programs to the fact that little children may miss school from time to time. Teachers should encourage parents to keep at home children who are ill and to take care of minor disturbances in the child's health. This procedure can prevent longer absences resulting from more serious complications and it also prevents exposure of other children to diseases. Teachers should also be alert to symptoms of fatigue and arrange frequent rest periods. A mid-morning snack might be well worth a few minutes' time also, as an energy restorer for undernourished children.

Frequent reviews should be a normal part of the first-grade program so that absentees can catch up with what has taken place. A daily special-help period for those just returning after absence will prevent discouragement and the loss of interest that is likely to occur when others have forged ahead.

To a child, a week's absence seems as long as a month's absence would seem to an adult. A special word of welcome will help to give the child the feeling of having been missed, and an explanation of what has happened in the interim will help him a great deal in getting back into the swing of things again. It is easy for a child to feel left out when he returns from an absence, as the following case illustrates.

Arthur missed a few weeks of school in the first grade on account of illness. Because the class was so crowded, the teacher gave his desk to a newcomer during his absence. When he returned to school, someone else was at his desk and no other seat was vacant. His teacher, nervous and overworked by such a crowded class, called in the principal, and together they commiserated as they discussed what to do. Arthur meanwhile stood by, embarrassed, shifting from one foot to the other, feeling that he was in some way to blame for all the trouble. At last, a kindergarten table and chair were brought in and he was installed in a corner of the room. The next morning, at home, he wept bitterly and refused to go to school, saying, "They don't want me there. I don't belong there any more. Someone else has my desk, and they're on a different book now." From that day on, Arthur failed to adjust and by the end of the year was so far behind that he had to repeat the grade.

Arthur's is an extreme case, fortunately, but many children feel strange and lost after an absence, even if they return to their own desks. A little special attention at this time to overcome the children's anxieties may prevent reading from becoming a problem—and prevent anxiety about reading from becoming an emotional block to further learning.

MENTAL RETARDATION

Children grow mentally at different rates and have greater or lesser potentialities for their final adult mental level. The course of mental growth corresponds in many ways with that of physical growth; both are modified, within limits, by the kind of nurture given during the period of growth. A child who has potentialities for being a tall adult, for example, may not reach the high stature possible for him if he suffers from severe malnutrition which stunts his growth. By good physical and mental hygiene, we may help children attain their maximum potentialities, both physical and mental.

Infants learn to talk at different rates in accordance with their mental growth. Mentally retarded children acquire language slowly. There are many other reasons for retardation in language besides a low intelligence, however, and every possible approach should be made to develop language in a child before assuming that he is mentally dull. Even if a child who is deficient in language is given an intelligence test and the test reveals low intelligence, the conclusion should not necessarily be drawn that the child is intellectually deficient. The child is low in whatever it is the test measures, and many intelligence tests (particularly group tests) are highly weighted with items that require the child to understand language and formulate or select a verbal reply. A psychologist skilled in interpreting intelligence tests can be very helpful to the teacher in such cases. He can give nonverbal tests for comparison with verbal ones and, insofar as possible, help distinguish the child who is truly mentally retarded from the one who only appears to be so because of language deficiency.

LINGUISTIC AND SOCIAL DEPRIVATION

Home background may affect the language competence of the child in many ways. The language that a child knows when he comes to school is a reflection of the environment in which he has lived. This environment includes the language of his home and neighborhood, plus whatever he may have picked up from radio or TV. The differences in language background are as great as the social and cultural differences which exist in adult society.

Foreign language in the home

Foreign language spoken in the home is a frequent cause of retardation in the use of English at school. Not all foreign-language backgrounds are the same, however, and not all of them have the same effect on a child's linguistic progress in English.

First, there is the child who has developed normal use of his native tongue in a cultured foreign home but who does not speak English. His ability to understand and formulate his own language may be average or superior, and such a child would have no language problem if he were to learn to read his native tongue. In learning to read English, however, he has the problem of acquiring a second language. Once he has mastered an essential English vocabulary of a few hundred words, has learned to formulate sentences in the new language, and has learned a few idioms, he should begin to make quite rapid progress. His problem is to learn to "think" in English without translating words back into his native tongue for meaning. As soon as such a child has mastered the primer vocabulary he is to read and can use the words in speaking, he usually has no further trouble and continues to learn simultaneously how to understand, speak, and read English.

Another child may have been exposed from infancy to two languages at the same time. If he is free from physical or emotional factors that would retard language growth and if he has intelligent, understanding parents who speak both languages fluently, the child may keep the languages separate and make good progress in each. He may not have quite as much proficiency in English as the child who speaks only English, but he may have a greater feeling for languages because of a heightened sensitivity to the nature of language patterns and the sounds of language.

A child may become easily confused, however, if he is exposed to a mixture of languages by parents who know only a little English and who lapse frequently and without warning into their native tongue when they cannot find the English words. Such a child learns to speak a patois that is neither English nor the foreign language. This pattern is likely to be reinforced by neighborhood contacts with other children of similar language background, since members of nationality groups tend to cluster together, particularly in larger urban areas. In school, where his foreign words and idioms will not be accepted, the child may try to learn English substitutes, but these may be misunderstood in turn by his family, especially by parents or older adults. Older brothers and sisters may help to break the way for bringing more English into the home, but the mother tongue remains in most cases the parents' means of communication. Children from such homes may or may not speak English with an accent derived from their parents' mother tongue, but they are likely to be retarded in their use of English in comparison with children from more favorable language backgrounds. They may borrow word order or idioms from their parents' language, and they will probably have a smaller English vocabulary than might otherwise be the case.

Adult classes in English and the Americanization programs which many communities offer for the adult foreign-born are helpful, since they make it possible for parents to improve the English heard by the child at home. In some cities there are junior first grades that are directed primarily toward helping children learn English before instruction in reading is begun.

Educational and socioeconomic level of the home and neighborhood

Even when English is the language spoken at home, there may be a serious deficiency of desirable language experience. Experiences with books, experiences of being read to, experiences of seeing adults read are rare or nonexistent in many homes. The language spoken, although English, may be nonstandard and thus unacceptable at school. Indeed, in many deprived homes language of any kind is used sparingly, reserved usually for discipline of children or for emotional tirades directed against other adults. The concept of relaxed and thoughtful exchange of ideas at a rational, verbal level is virtually unknown.

Frequently found in such a nonverbal home background is a cluster of attitudes and emotions that further handicap the child. Adults who themselves had slight—and, in many cases, unpleasant—experiences in school are not likely to create for their children an environment of love for books and learning or of respect for schools and teachers. Nor are they able to help their children, even if they want to, by providing adequate models of spoken language or by giving help of any kind with school lessons.

In addition to these handicaps of family background, the dynamics of our communities are such that the neighborhood in most cases simply reinforces the values of the home. In many lower-class neighborhoods, both schools and teachers are regarded as authority symbols, representing a hostile superordinate society. Even success in school and approval by the teacher are likely to be shunned as signs of capitulation to the enemy. As for language models, the speech of other residents of the neighborhood is not likely to be greatly different from that of any of the individual families in it. In fact, mastery of the neighborhood patois is a mark of belonging, so that children have a strong motivation for not learning many of the language skills the school will try to teach. The small child who is a product of this setting comes to school burdened with disadvantages that are both psychological and linguistic.

It would seem that the mass media—especially television, which reaches into nearly all homes of every socioeconomic class—might tend to equalize the differences in preschool language experience. It has been established, for instance, that television increases the vocabulary of the preschool child.[2] But to date television seems to have had no more success than radio in altering basic speech patterns or in erasing differences in verbal achievement. A recent study, made in Detroit[3] as part of the Great Cities School Improvement Program, revealed the wide differences still prevailing in 1960 between the verbal skills of vast numbers of underprivileged children living in low socioeconomic urban areas and the language achievement levels assumed for moderate or even minimal success in schoolroom reading and language classes.

[2] See Chapter 1, pages 13-15.
[3] Dominic R. Thomas, *Oral Language Sentence Structure and Vocabulary of Kindergarten Children Living in Low Socio-Economic Urban Areas.* Unpublished Ph.D. dissertation, Wayne State University, 1962.

Helping the linguistically handicapped

Teachers are becoming increasingly aware of the kinds of problems faced by children coming to school with inadequate language experience. Considerable effort is being devoted by educators to devising materials and activities that will in some way compensate for language deprivation and, if possible, for meagerness of experiences of all kinds. Publicly supported nursery schools as well as kindergartens are recommended to fill the "emotional, motivational, and verbal gaps" for underprivileged children between the ages of three and a half and six years.[4] Where such a program is not possible, small groups that help the child to form a warm, personal attachment for the teacher are suggested, along with a program of activities designed to provide as wide a variety as possible of verbal experiences, including listening to stories told by the teacher and just "chatting" in the classroom.

Opportunities to become familiar with books are equally important. Children who have been deprived of normal pre-reading experiences need special help if they are to build the emotional security with books that leads to a desire to read. They should be encouraged to experiment with books just as other infants and preschool children experiment with such materials in their homes. They should have an opportunity to explore picture books, to turn the pages at will, to feel them, to pat them, and to express individually whatever ideas the pictures suggest. They should not be scolded for tearing, if they have never turned pages before, or for crumpling, if they do not yet understand how thin and fragile the paper in books can be. Reading aloud to them in small groups as often as possible is a good idea. Such reading needs to be accompanied by the explanation that the printing under the pictures tells the reader what to say. Simple stories should be read and reread until the children have been able to memorize them. Then they may enjoy the experience of looking through

[4] Esther Milner, "A Study of the Relationship Between Reading Readiness in Grade One School Children and Patterns of Parent-Child Interaction," *Child Development*, 22 (June 1951), 95-112.

a book while mentally reconstructing the language heard for each picture. In short, they need an opportunity to build up—not too fast—the concepts of book care, picture interpretation, language understandings, and the joyful anticipation of learning to read that children from book-loving homes have already had an opportunity to acquire.

BIBLIOGRAPHY

Axline, Virginia Mae. *Play Therapy*. Boston: Houghton Mifflin Company, 1947. Discusses the use of play therapy and group therapy to help maladjusted children. Illustrative material from case studies shows how a teacher or psychologist can help children to work their own way out of the difficult realities in which they may be forced to live.

Brazziel, William F., and Terrell, Mary. "For First-Graders: A Good Start in School," *Elementary School Journal*, 62 (April 1962), 352-355. Compares readiness scores of children who participated in a six-week readiness program that included guided parental help with scores of children in three control groups. All children in experimental and control groups were from a deprived semi-rural area in Tennessee. The experiment was designed to discover ways of helping underprivileged children at the first-grade level.

Brock, Frederick W. "Two Eyes Can Be Worse Than One," *Education*, 77 (April 1957), 501-504. Explains the problems of binocular vision—how it develops or fails to develop and the symptoms displayed by children who may have some difficulty in using two eyes together.

Bryngelson, Bryng, and Glaspey, Esther. *Improving Articulation*. Teacher's Manual to accompany Speech Improvement Cards, Revised Edition. Chicago: Scott, Foresman and Company, 1962. Suggestions for helping the classroom teacher motivate and direct the development of good speech. Focuses on the improvement of speech of children with functional articulatory disorders.

Eames, Thomas H. "Visual Handicaps to Reading," *Boston University Journal of Education*, 141 (February 1959), 1-35.

Explanation by a medical doctor of visual anomalies and their effect on schoolroom performance. Technical terms are used, but an attempt is made to explain them in lay language.

Kasdon, Lawrence M. "Reading and the Bilingual Child," *Challenge and Experiment in Reading,* International Reading Association Conference Proceedings, 7 (1962), 90-92. Discusses the various kinds of problems the bilingual child may have in interpreting stories from standard commercial readers. Based on the writer's experience in Hawaii but applicable to a wide range of problems arising from foreign-language or foreign-culture background.

Lieben, Beatrice. "Attitudes, Platitudes, and Conferences in Teacher-Parent Relations Involving the Child with a Reading Problem," *Elementary School Journal,* 58 (February 1958), 279-286. Suggests how the teacher can work with the parent to help children with reading problems.

Milner, Esther. "A Study of the Relationship Between Reading Readiness in Grade One School Children and Patterns of Parent-Child Interaction," *Child Development,* 22 (June 1951), 95-112. Examines the hypothesis that good reading performance is related to "high" family social status.

Monroe, Marion. *Children Who Cannot Read.* Chicago: University of Chicago Press, 1932. Study of 415 children who had severe reading difficulties, with an analysis of the causes of their reading problems as seen in the reading clinic of the Institute for Juvenile Research in Chicago. Presents a statistical comparison of problems of these poor readers with a control group of average readers.

Robinson, Helen M. *Why Pupils Fail in Reading.* Chicago: University of Chicago Press, 1946. A comprehensive examination and appraisal of the significance of various possible causes of serious reading retardation. Considers home conditions, other environmental factors, and inappropriate teaching procedures. Good background information for kindergarten and first-grade teachers who try to prevent serious retardation by keeping alert to the warning signals.

Spache, George D., and Tillman, Chester E. "A Comparison of the Visual Profiles of Retarded and Non-Retarded Readers," *Journal of Developmental Reading*, 5 (Winter 1962), 101-109. Study of visual differences between retarded and non-retarded readers. Presents evidence that fusion difficulties often characterize poor readers.

Thomas, Dominic R. *Oral Language Sentence Structure and Vocabulary of Kindergarten Children Living in Low Socio-Economic Urban Areas*. Unpublished Ph.D. dissertation, Wayne State University, 1962. One of the few studies that have been made of sentence patterns used by children living in poor urban areas.

Van Riper, Charles, and Butler, Katherine G. *Speech in the Elementary Classroom*. New York: Harper & Row, 1955. Techniques and methods for helping children improve articulation and develop fluency. Primarily for the classroom teacher who is responsible for both developmental and corrective speech work with her pupils.

chapter eight

Organizing For Action

The preceding chapters have presented a variety of activities that can be used to develop basic reading-readiness skills. Methods of strengthening auditory, visual, and interpretative skills have been described, as well as devices for relating these skills to the specific tasks of interpreting printed language.

Since some kind of reading-readiness activity has become customary in almost all schools, there is little need to stress the importance of including such work as a part of the total program for learning to read. The problem with which most schools are at present struggling is how best to adjust the pre-reading program to the needs of each of the individuals being taught. Such questions as the following need to be answered: How can pupils be most appropriately grouped for various kinds of skill-building activities? How can grouping be made flexible enough to accommodate ever changing rates of growth? How can levels of readiness best be identified? How can the curriculum best be adjusted to the unique growth patterns of each individual?

Answers to these questions are not easily determined. They lie to some extent in the area of evaluation and to some extent in the area of school-system organization. Evaluation procedures—both informal ones, such as those suggested in Chapter 2, and the more formal standardized tests described later in this chapter—provide information about readiness of an individual for a certain level of work and about suitable groupings for certain kinds of skill-building activities. They help the teacher to know *who* needs *what kind* of instruction *when*. But evaluative devices do not tell the teacher *how* to proceed within those limits, nor do they provide the organizational setting within which grouping and instruction take place. The organizational setting itself needs to provide the opportunity for making the best use of information gained from the evaluative procedures.

Some types of school organization provide more freedom and more flexibility than others. In an instructional program where little use is made of evaluative devices, relatively little flexibility in the organizational system is required in order to use the information available about individual pupils. If more extensive use is made of a variety of evaluative devices so that a great deal is known about each pupil, then the system of organization needs to be proportionately more flexible if the instructional program is to be shaped to meet the known needs of individual pupils.

This chapter describes techniques of evaluation, systems of organization, and the relation of both to planning the reading program at the pre-reading and beginning-reading levels.

TECHNIQUES OF EVALUATION

Today more than ever before a teacher can accumulate a wide variety of information about each of her pupils. Not only does she have guidance from the insights of child psychology and child development to assist her in interpreting the child's everyday behavior, but she has available also a wide range of test instruments, from informal to formal. Prepared tests include tests of intelligence, tests of academic readiness, and tests of various types of sensory acuity and discrimination. In interpreting the scores of any of these tests, the teacher may rely on innumerable studies relating to personality factors, to child development, to the learning process, to the nature of mental and physical growth of children, to language development, and to social and emotional development.

Evaluative techniques that are frequently used with children at pre-reading and beginning-reading levels include (1) informal observation; (2) informal tests; and (3) formal, or standardized, tests.

Informal observation

Many aspects of a child's behavior may be observed in the normal course of classroom activity. Of this observable behavior, a surprisingly large part has some relevance to reading readiness. Such behavior needs only to be carefully observed and then recorded in such a way that it can be interpreted satisfactorily, in order to provide the teacher with a springboard for planning her first cycle of pre-reading activities.

Language behavior is, of course, of greatest importance. Some of the ways in which the child's use of language can be recorded and interpreted were mentioned in Chapter 2. The most useful kinds of information to record are the quality of ideas that seems to characterize the child's thinking, the way in which he defines words, his ability to verbalize his ideas, and the command he has of English sentence structure. From these kinds of information, the teacher should be able to form a reasonably clear picture of how the child thinks and what his general level of language competence may be. If the teacher has an opportunity to record specific illustrations of the child's speech, she will gain still further insight into the nature of his special strengths and weaknesses in using the English language.

Other areas of observation provide other types of insights

into skills related to the process of learning to read. These other areas include social-emotional adjustment, interpretative skills, and visual, auditory and motor skills.

In noting social-emotional adjustment the teacher will want to observe such things as whether the child is co-operative, whether he seems to be adjusted to a group learning situation, whether he is able to give attention to a story being told, and whether he enjoys looking at pictures and books.

Ability to interpret story material may be observed by noting how well the child is able to recognize the main idea in a picture story, how well he is able to make inferences or anticipate outcomes, how well he is able to form associations, and how well he is able to remember details.

Visual skill may be observed in a child's ability to compare and contrast the shapes and sizes of three-dimensional objects and the shapes and sizes of objects in pictures. Auditory discrimination may be checked by noting a child's ability to distinguish among sounds, especially sounds that occur in spoken language. Exercises that require the child to distinguish between initial sounds in words are helpful as a diagnostic device as well as an instructional procedure. Motor skills should be observed, especially at the level of large muscle coordination. Such control may be observed in a large variety of activities during the day. In fact, any of the activities developed by the teacher for developing muscular coordination will provide a good check on individual levels of muscular skill.

The teacher's role in testing

To obtain a more precise measure of what she can reasonably expect from each child, the teacher may want to use tests to determine not only degree of readiness for reading but also general intelligence. Such scores can help a teacher to group children and to time and choose pre-reading activities. Later on, tests may help to determine the effectiveness of the pre-reading program and the degree of readiness for actual reading.

In general, there are two main types of tests used to

measure skills, abilities and understandings. Some tests have been standardized by being administered to large numbers of children. Other tests are informal ones designed by the teacher for a specific purpose and given only to the children in her own classroom. Both types are valuable, and the teacher who knows both how to use standardized tests and how to create an informal test for a purpose of her own may check her personal appraisal of children's abilities against objective test data.

One of the most difficult problems a teacher faces in administering tests is that of changing her own role from teacher to examiner. As a teacher, she tries to help a child to learn. She tries to offer the kind of assistance best calculated to help him think his way through to the correct answer. If necessary, she simplifies a question or repeats it or rearranges it in some way to help the pupil to understand. She may call attention to certain facts or to relationships among facts, or she may demonstrate the fallacy in a first approach and encourage a different attack on the problem. She is constantly adjusting to the pupil's personality and to his individual needs and special problems.

As an examiner, the teacher assumes a different role. She can no longer make allowance for individual differences. The nature of a standardized test is such that it must be administered in the same way to all pupils regardless of the difficulties that individual pupils may have with particular items. Even the exact words the teacher may say are specified in the test manual, and any deviation from prescribed procedures will invalidate the test results. The teacher cannot help the pupil who doesn't quite understand the question, the pupil who needs the reassurance of knowing whether or not he has the right answer, or the pupil who wants a little extra guidance. Even helping the slow pupil by allowing him a little more time may be forbidden. No adjustment of any kind to individual needs may be permitted to interfere with the prescribed method of administering the test.

All of this emphasis on precision, however, by no means indicates that the test atmosphere need be anxious or strained. To the contrary, the teacher should establish an easy, friendly atmosphere before she begins testing and do everything possible to maintain this atmosphere at all times. She should motivate the child to do the best he can by using any ingenious means she can devise, always short of altering the prescribed procedure.

Administering an informal test allows the teacher more flexibility and more opportunity to adjust to the needs of individual pupils than does the formal test. For example, an informal test may not be timed, allowing the teacher to give slower pupils adequate time to do the best work of which they are capable. Other adjustments to individual needs also may be possible. When a teacher has designed her own test, she will naturally be in a position to use her own judgment as to how much help she may give during the administration of the test. She should be careful, however, even in an informal testing situation, not to let her natural urge to teach interfere with the process of making a fair and valid measurement.

Informal tests

Tests of an informal type, constructed by the teacher, may be either diagnostic or evaluative or both. In any case, they have one distinctive quality that can rarely be obtained in a commercially prepared, standardized test: they focus directly on just those skills the teacher has been emphasizing in the classroom. As evaluative instruments, such tests give the teacher an opportunity to find out how well individual pupils have mastered particular skills and how pupils can best be grouped in relation to their achievement levels.

At the pre-reading level, many developmental activities serve the double purpose of building skills and checking on mastery level. Many of the activities suggested in this book, especially in Chapters 4, 5, and 6, can be used for such double duty, serving both as developmental activities and as informal tests of various skills. The teacher may, of course, add items similar to those suggested in order to produce a more adequate check of the skill area on which she wishes to focus. In addition to the suggestions in this book, many helpful ideas for informal testing may be found in pupils' reading-readiness texts. In order to transform a book "exercise" into an informal test, the teacher need only note the number of items a child has marked correctly and record this as a "score" in her record book (not on the child's page).

In informal testing, the entire class serves as a "standard" against which each child's work can be compared. The top fourth of the scores may be rated as "high"; the bottom fourth as "low"; and the middle half as "average." Those children whose work is relatively low may be given extra practice until they have mastered the skill measured by the test. Scores should be kept confidential and tests treated simply as games in which it is fun to do the best that one can.

In interpreting the test scores, the teacher should remember that a child's score on an informal test, though low or high as compared with the average for the entire class, is not necessarily low or high for that particular child or for that particular age group. For example, a child who is only five in a classroom of six-year-old children may make a score on some test below the scores of most of his classmates. If he were in a classroom of children his own age, however, his score might be average or better. On the other hand, a seven-year-old child repeating first grade may score high in certain skills, yet if his score could be compared with the scores of seven-year-olds who had gone on to second grade, it might be considerably below the average. Informal tests should be interpreted with all personal data about the pupil in mind. Nevertheless, for teaching purposes, it is helpful to find those youngsters in a class who are unable to make certain types of discriminations, to do certain kinds of thinking, or to perform certain tasks, and to be able to measure their progress, from week to week, in each specific area.

Formal standardized tests

The standardized tests most useful to teachers of beginning reading are tests of intelligence and tests of something referred to as "reading readiness." Since the two types of tests serve somewhat different purposes it may be helpful to discuss them separately.

Intelligence tests. Intelligence tests are in general use in public schools throughout the country, but they are administered less frequently in the lower grades than in the upper ones. In kindergarten and first grade, especially, the use of intelligence tests involves certain practical difficulties. The most reliable way of testing the intelligence of very young children is through the use of an individually administered test, but this immediately raises a problem in most schools. The classroom teacher is not usually trained in psychological testing, and, even if she were, she lacks sufficient time to administer an individual intelligence test to each pupil in her class. The ideal solution is for the school system to provide a specialist to administer individual tests, but few school systems can afford to provide this kind of special assistance. Sometimes problem cases may be referred to the school psychologist for such testing, but the possibility of having such scores for a whole class is remote in most instances.

The scores from group intelligence tests are usually less reliable than the scores from individually administered tests. For most teachers, however, I.Q.'s obtained from group tests are the only intelligence scores available. In using group tests, it is wise to remember that the results are only approximate. No two intelligence tests are likely to give the same I.Q. for the same child: the difference in I.Q.'s from test to test, administered to the same child at approximately the same time, will often be ten points or more. Thus, an I.Q. should be taken to represent a range rather than an exact point on a scale. So interpreted, it can be valuable to the teacher in several ways.

1) Most intelligence tests show something called "mental age." This information gives the teacher an objective rating of the child's mental development at the time of school entrance, or at whatever time the test may be administered. Children of widely differing chronological ages may be of the same mental age. For example, both a five-year-old child and a seven-year-old child may have a mental age of

six. Applying the "rule" that a mental age of five and a half to six and a half is appropriate for beginning to learn to read, both children may be judged ready for reading.

Mental age alone, however, is hardly adequate as a sole criterion of reading readiness. Such factors as motor skill, auditory and visual discrimination, motivation, and emotional maturity may be equally important.

2) The intelligence score helps the teacher to determine the *rate* at which the child is developing. A five-year-old and a seven-year-old, both with the mental age of six, obviously are not learning at the same rate. The five-year-old apparently has a greater capacity to learn and is learning at a considerably faster rate. By providing information about rate of mental growth, intelligence test scores can help the teacher to maintain appropriate groupings in her class, giving her a better idea than she might otherwise have about how rapidly each pupil will be able to move from one instructional level to the next. A teacher would not, for example, expect a pupil with an I.Q. of 85 to progress as rapidly as a pupil with an I.Q. of 120.

3) Some intelligence tests serve diagnostic purposes— especially those tests that give both verbal and performance scores. The amount and kind of discrepancy between these two scores may reveal the degree to which linguistic experience is affecting an overall intelligence score.

Some of the most frequently used intelligence tests, both group and individual, are described below.

The Revised Stanford-Binet Scale.[1]　This test, designed to be administered individually by a psychologist, may be used with any child over two. It measures primarily the kind of intelligence that contributes to success in academic achievement. At the four-, five-, and six-year levels the items focus on such skills as vocabulary, naming objects from memory, discriminating among forms, rote memory, memory for sentences, seeing likenesses and differences, finding missing parts, and maze tracing. A number of these

[1] Lewis M. Terman and Maud A. Merrill, *Revised Stanford-Binet Scale.* Boston: Houghton Mifflin Company, 1937.

items require the kinds of visual, language, and interpretative abilities that the child will need when he learns to read. A psychologist may also use the performance on this test as a basis for determining certain types of emotional disturbances.

Wechsler Intelligence Scale for Children.[2] This test also is designed to be administered to individual pupils by a clinician. It may be used with children between the ages of five and fifteen. There are fifteen scores derived from both verbal and performance subtests. The verbal parts of the test are: information, comprehension, arithmetic, similarities, vocabulary, and digit-span (optional). The performance subtests include picture completion, picture arrangement, block design, object assembly, mazes (optional), and coding.

The Wechsler differs from other intelligence tests in that it is not based on the concept of mental age. Instead, the I.Q. score is expressed in terms of mean and standard deviation of the age group. The standardization samples are considered to be a good cross section of white American children, although the test does not sample as wide a range of performance among the dullest of the lowest age group as does the Stanford-Binet. In general, the Stanford-Binet and the Wechsler (WISC) correlate fairly highly—about .8 —and are equally useful as predictors of academic success. The WISC has the advantage of providing two scores, a verbal and a performance score, thus making it possible to compare a child's verbal intelligence with his nonverbal problem-solving ability.

S.R.A. Primary Mental Abilities.[3] This is a group test (formerly called *Tests of Primary Mental Abilities for Ages 5 and 6*) that may be used by the classroom teacher beginning in the kindergarten. There are five subscores—verbal, perceptual, quantitative, motor, and spatial—and a total

[2] David Wechsler, *Wechsler Intelligence Scale for Children.* New York: Psychological Corporation, 1949.
[3] L. L. Thurstone and Thelma Gwinn Thurstone, *S.R.A. Primary Mental Abilities* (Grades K-2). Chicago: Science Research Associates, Inc., 1953-1958.

score. The test consists of pictures to be marked by the children. Because of the separate scores, the test shows the pattern of abilities of a given child. A child who has an aptitude for numbers but a deficiency in language, for example, will probably score relatively high in the quantitative test items and relatively low in verbal items. The test is to be administered in two sessions, one day apart.

California Test of Mental Maturity.[4]   This is a group test that gives three scores: verbal, nonverbal, and total. The total score provides a single measure of intelligence, while the separate scores make it possible to identify children who may have special ability or special problems in either language or nonlanguage areas. The subtests are designed to measure memory, spatial relations, reasoning, vocabulary, visual and auditory acuity, and motor coordination. The tests of visual and auditory acuity and the tests of motor coordination are useful for identifying difficulties that pupils may have in these areas.

Kuhlman-Anderson Intelligence Tests.[5]   This is a group test containing a number of subtests, each of which is scored separately in terms of mental age. The median mental-age score of all the tests is the final score. Since the teacher can tell at a glance on which tests a child's score is high or low, this battery of tests has diagnostic value as well as value as an indicator of general intelligence. The tests are easily administered and easily scored.

Lorge-Thorndike Intelligence Tests.[6]   This is a group test that calls for nonverbal responses only, at the kindergarten to first-grade level. The following behaviors are tested:

[4] Elizabeth T. Sullivan, Willis W. Clark, and Ernest W. Tiegs, *California Test of Mental Maturity* (Grades K-1). Monterey, Calif.: California Test Bureau, 1957.
[5] F. Kuhlman and Rose G. Anderson, *Kuhlman-Anderson Intelligence Tests*, Sixth Edition (for kindergarten, first grade, and up). Princeton, N.J.: Personnel Press, Inc., 1952.
[6] Irving Lorge and Robert L. Thorndike, *Lorge-Thorndike Intelligence Tests* (Grades K-1). Boston: Houghton Mifflin Company, 1957.

dealing with abstract and general concepts; interpreting and using symbols; dealing with relationships among concepts and symbols; flexibility in organization of concepts and symbols; using experience in new patterns; using power rather than speed in working with abstract materials. In general, the purpose of the test is to discover the child's ability to work with ideas and with the relationships among ideas. The tests are easily administered and scored. Spanish directions are available for the nonverbal K-1 tests.

Detroit Beginning First-Grade Intelligence Test.[7] This group test consists of a booklet of pictures which the children mark according to verbal directions. Brief and easy to administer, it measures intelligence in terms of mental age.

Detroit Kindergarten Test.[8] This is an individual test that consists of a booklet of pictures which the examiner marks in accordance with the child's responses to his instructions. Designed for five-year-old children, it is brief and easily administered, and thus useful for a quick screening. Because of its brevity, however, doubtful cases need further study.

Davis-Eells Games.[9] This is a group test constructed entirely of pictures. The examiner, who is considered to be the "game leader," reads the directions, which are phrased in colloquial language. Each test is presented as a "game" with emphasis on maintaining an atmosphere of play and relaxation. The test was designed to be as nearly as possible culturally fair: that is, to reduce the effects of socioeconomic differences on test scores. Research to date, however, suggests that the scores from these "games" show about the same amount of difference between high and low

---

[7] Anna M. Engel and Harry J. Baker, *Detroit Beginning First-Grade Intelligence Test* (for first-grade entrants). New York: Harcourt, Brace and World, Inc., 1937.

[8] Harry J. Baker and H. J. Kaufmann, *Detroit Kindergarten Test* (for kindergarten entrants). New York: Harcourt, Brace and World, Inc., 1925.

[9] Allison Davis and Kenneth Eells, *Davis-Eells Test of General Intelligence or Problem Solving Ability* (Grades 1-2). New York: Harcourt, Brace and World, Inc., 1953.

socioeconomic groups as do the scores from the *California Test of Mental Maturity*.

Readiness tests. The other type of standardized test which, along with the intelligence test, is especially useful to the kindergarten or first-grade teacher is the readiness test. Reading-readiness tests are designed to measure skills especially needed in reading. Some of the items in readiness tests are similar to those in intelligence tests, and there is a certain amount of overlapping in the areas tested—especially in the areas of language and reasoning. In general, however, the reading-readiness tests focus on items that are dependent to some degree on training, and thus they are different from the intelligence tests which attempt to measure potential for learning rather than learning. Reading-readiness tests include such items as letter and word matching, reading letters, writing one's name, discriminating among pictures, remembering a story, and responding to rhymes. The use of a reading-readiness test combined with an intelligence test, plus informal observation of the kind that has already been suggested, gives a teacher a basis for grouping children during the pre-reading period. Some of the readiness tests are described in the following paragraphs.

Metropolitan Readiness Tests.[10]   These are group tests designed to measure readiness for reading, arithmetic, and writing. The tests are easily administered and scored, and they provide the teacher with a wider range of information than would a reading-readiness test alone. Items include language comprehension, observation of likenesses, drawing, and comprehension of numbers.

Lee-Clark Reading Readiness Test.[11]   This group test is brief and easily administered, consisting of the following

[10] Gertrude H. Hildreth and Nellie L. Griffiths, *Metropolitan Readiness Tests* (for end of kindergarten and for first-grade entrants). New York: Harcourt, Brace and World, Inc., 1950.
[11] J. Murray Lee and Willis W. Clark, *Lee-Clark Reading Readiness Test* (Grades K-1). Monterey, Calif.: California Test Bureau, 1951. (Identical to test copyrighted in 1943.)

types of items: matching letters; crossing out one of four letters which is unlike the other three; marking pictures according to verbal directions; marking the one of four printed words that matches a given word. The test is thus limited to items requiring either visual discrimination of printed words or the following of verbal directions. Teachers who are interested in measuring these particular skills will find this test useful.

Gates Reading Readiness Tests.[12] This test combines group and individual sections. The five subtests are: Picture Directions, Word Matching, Word-Card Matching, Rhyming, and Reading Letters and Numbers. Norms provided separately for each subtest enable the teacher to use the test for diagnostic purposes and also allow her to omit one or more of the subtests and still obtain a rough measure of readiness.

Monroe Reading Aptitude Tests.[13] Like the preceding one, this test combines group and individual sections. It is designed to measure five areas of ability important for success in reading: visual abilities (recognizing orientation of forms, following a path with the eyes, and drawing forms from memory); auditory abilities (discriminating words heard, sound blending, and memory of story); motor abilities (speed of tapping, steadiness of tracing, and ability to write one's name); articulation (accuracy and speed); and language (vocabulary, speed of classification, and sentence length). These tests are designed primarily for diagnostic purposes, in order to discover children who may need special help in certain areas before they begin reading instruction. Also included is a brief series of tests for hand, eye, and foot preferences.

Mastery tests. Still another type of test is the "mastery" test. Mastery tests indicate to what degree a pupil has

---

[12] Arthur I. Gates, *Gates Reading Readiness Tests* (Grade 1). New York: Bureau of Publications, Teachers College, 1939-1942.
[13] Marion Monroe, *Reading Aptitude Tests* (Grades K-1). Boston: Houghton Mifflin Company, 1935.

mastered a certain skill or ability at a certain level of difficulty. They differ from standardized tests of achievement in that they do not attempt to measure a pupil's maximum ability, but only his mastery of material at a certain level. A general-achievement or reading-achievement test, on the other hand, is designed to measure the upper limits of a pupil's ability. This is done by including some items of sufficient difficulty to stump even the ablest pupil in the group. The point at which a pupil "fails" such a test thus indicates presumably the maximum achievement of which that pupil is capable.

When scores from a standardized general-achievement test or a standardized reading-achievement test are plotted, with the number of pupils on the vertical axis and the scores on the horizontal axis, then the resulting curve is something approaching the well-known normal distribution curve, as shown in the figure below. The shape of this curve indi-

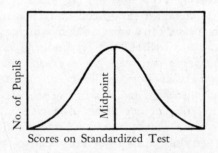

Scores on Standardized Test

cates that the majority of pupils fall at or near the national norm for the grade or level being tested, with a few pupils scoring considerably below the norm and a few scoring considerably above the norm. The curve resulting from the plotting of mastery-test scores in the same manner is different. The mastery-test curve, as shown in the next figure, is skewed sharply, with most scores piling up toward the right-hand side. This skewing results from the fact that the test is not administered until the class, or ability group, has successfully completed the comparable instructional material. It is also understood that the test will

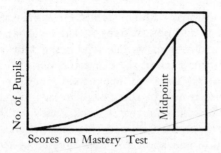

include no items that exceed in difficulty the level already reached in the instruction. Thus, if the group or class has successfully completed the instructional unit or units covered by the test, most of the pupils can be expected to answer correctly a large percentage of the test items. The mastery-test score tells the teacher whether or not each pupil has acquired the skills needed for attempting the next level in the reading program. Mastery-test scores do not indicate how far a pupil's achievement level may lie beyond the instructional level. To obtain that information the teacher needs to administer a standardized reading-achievement test.

Mastery tests may be constructed by the teacher, or they may be obtained from some of the publishers of reading programs.[14]

SYSTEMS OF ORGANIZATION

The foregoing paragraphs have described some of the evaluative devices which the teacher may want to use in

[14]See, for example, Marion Monroe and Helen M. Robinson, *Basic Reading Tests*, Sixties Edition, to accompany the *New Basic Readers*. Chicago: Scott, Foresman and Company, 1962. Scores from these tests may be used for two purposes: grouping and diagnosis. The total score provides an indication of where any one child in a group stands in relation to the total group and in relation to the national norm for pupils who have completed a given level of the reading program. The subtest scores provide a profile of the pupil's relative strengths and weaknesses in specific skill areas. Interpretation of the subtest scores thus makes possible diagnosis and further analysis of individual problems.

getting acquainted with her pupils. How she uses the results of these tests and observations will depend on the kind of organizational system within which she works. The next section explains some of the characteristics of organizational systems that are currently being used.

Organization may be thought of in two ways: (1) as the horizontal organization that a teacher uses within the classroom as a basis for grouping for instruction, and (2) as the vertical organization that is designated as a school-wide system for moving children upward through the school curriculum from the beginning year to ultimate completion of a certain body of studies. Since the grouping for instruction within the classroom depends on the nature of the school-wide vertical organization, the principal types of vertical organization need to be considered first. There are in use at the present time in the United States primarily two systems of vertical organization: the graded organization and the nongraded organization.

Graded organization

The graded system is essentially a system in which each pupil is assigned, according to his chronological age, to a specific grade level, such as kindergarten or Grade 1. The work of each level is customarily described in a curriculum guide, which prescribes the level of achievement expected of pupils by the time they have completed the designated grade or year. At the end of each school year, the teacher is expected to have brought her pupils to the designated achievement level in each of the skill or content areas which are a part of the prescribed curriculum. In theory, she may retain for a repetition of the entire year's work any pupil who has not reached the designated level. In practice, however, such retentions are rare—especially at the kindergarten-primary level—and in most cases are unofficially, if not officially, discouraged. The term *social promotion* is used to describe the moving of children from one grade to the next whether or not they have reached the achievement level designated as a criterion for such promotion.

Thus, in almost all cases, the graded system may be said to be one in which a pupil is assigned to a grade level in accordance with his chronological age, in which the work of the grade consists of a predetermined curriculum designated as appropriate to that grade, and in which the pupil's mastery of the skills at that particular level is not the principal factor in his promotion to the next grade. In order to meet the wide range of achievements in a grade, teachers usually divide the pupils into smaller "ability groups" for instruction. Three such groups are perhaps the maximum that are manageable in one grade.

Nongraded organization

In a nongraded system, the pupil is placed in a large group that includes a range of ages. In many cases, all of the pupils within a relatively wide range of achievement are placed in a unit referred to as a nongraded primary unit. Within this large group, the pupil is assigned to special small groups according to his readiness level in specific content or skill areas. A nongraded organization permits greater flexibility of grouping than can be attained in a graded organization. The level of difficulty of the instructional material is indicated not in terms of grade level but in terms of the skills being taught. When a child is ready to proceed to a more advanced level of work, he is encouraged to do so, regardless of his chronological age or of calendar intervals. He may move upward more rapidly than he would in a graded system, or he may move less rapidly; but he will not be pushed ahead of his own ability to cope with the material being taught nor will he be held back if he is able to move ahead. The concept of "continuous progress" is viewed as the goal of this system of organization. The problem of promotion or nonpromotion arises when a transition to a graded segment of the school system is required. At such a transition point, the same problems of promotion procedure must be faced as with the graded system of organization.

Within the segment of the school system in which the nongraded procedure is followed, a pupil progresses continually at his own optimum rate, with mastery of skills and concepts at any given level used as the criterion for moving on to the next higher level.

GETTING STARTED

Regardless of the organizational system, the first days of school are the days of getting acquainted. Each teacher faces approximately the same type of problem—finding out as much as she can about each of her pupils. This process includes finding out where they are in social development, where they are in language development, where they are in emotional development, what the range of their experiences may be, how rapidly they are capable of learning, and how much they have already learned.

All of these areas of information may be tapped first of all through informal observation. Testing of a more formal type may wait until teacher and pupils have had an opportunity to get used to each other.

As instruction progresses, various day-to-day activities begin to provide opportunity for informal testing. Skill in speaking, skill in listening, skill in dealing with ideas, motor coordination, visual and auditory skills—all these and many more skills which are vital as bases for learning to read may be tested informally, without any awareness on the part of the children that they are being tested. These informal tests can provide a basis for grouping for the first pre-reading activities.

When teacher and pupils have had an opportunity to get used to each other and when pupils appear to feel relatively secure in their new environment, standardized tests may successfully be administered. In most schools, graded or nongraded, a general intelligence test is helpful, although, as has been pointed out, care must be taken not to make a rigid interpretation of the results. In addition to the intelligence test, standardized reading-readiness tests may be administered as soon as the teacher feels a need to compare the performance level of her pupils with that of pupils in other schools and in other parts of the country. The standardized tests provide norms in various areas and, therefore, are helpful in determining which instructional materials may be suitable for which pupils and which groups of pupils.

Using the results of evaluation: problems

When some or all of the evaluative devices suggested have been administered and scored, it will be apparent that the levels of instruction for which children in a given class are ready vary widely. Teachers are especially sensitive to this problem, although even they may not realize the full extent of the variability. A study conducted by the University of Michigan[15] in the public schools of Ferndale, Michigan, revealed a range of several years in mental abilities at any given chronological age, no matter how early children were tested. Some children of five and a half had a mental age of seven. Others with a chronological age of nine also had a mental age of seven. The twelve-year-old group included pupils with a mental age of sixteen and a half and pupils with a mental age of nine—a range of seven years.

In another study,[16] first-grade entrants with a chronological age range from five years, nine months to seven years, four months were found to have a range in mental age at that time from three years, ten months to eight years, four months. The spread was, in fact, four and a half years. The authors viewed the group studied as being very much like those in most middle-class schools across the country.

Thus the teacher who has conscientiously used an adequate battery of evaluative devices with her beginning class can count on finding in the group a mental-age range of approximately four and a half years. If the chronological ages are similar to those reported in the study just mentioned, then she may well find a child with a mental age of three years, ten months and a child with a mental age

[15] Warren A. Ketcham and Rondeau G. Lafitte, Jr., "How Well Are They Learning?" *Educational Leadership*, 16 (March 1959), 337-341, 350.
[16] John I. Goodlad and Robert H. Anderson, *The Nongraded Elementary School*. New York: Harcourt, Brace and World, Inc., 1959.

of eight years, four months sitting side by side.

Intra-class grouping provides a solution in the early stages of pre-reading instruction. However, the vastly differing rates at which these children learn soon raises the question of appropriate regroupings. In graded school systems, teachers are urged in almost all cases to keep the chronological age group together. This means that all pupils, regardless of mental age and regardless of rate of development, are expected to be ready to move on to a second year of school at the end of the first. Parents as well as administrators have sometimes been known to blame the teacher who was not able to bring all her pupils to this predetermined level of readiness for the next grade.

At one time, people hoped that holding children of a chronological age group together at the beginning stages of learning to read would enable them all to reach the same level of achievement later on as the result of schoolroom instruction. Such a hope was based on a misunderstanding of both the nature of mental growth and the effects of education. The range of individual differences actually increases as chronological age increases; and education, far from narrowing the gap between low and high achievers, widens it, since the more able learners make more effective use of whatever instruction is offered. Furthermore, the better the instruction, the farther and faster the differences increase. In most cases, the range in intellectual readiness to learn is as large as or larger than the number indicating the grade level. Reading is a consistent part of the total picture of mental growth. The range in reading age at each stage of development parallels the range in mental age.[17]

In any type of organization there are wide ranges of individual differences. In a group of children having the same *age*, the teacher must adjust to widely differing achievement levels. In a group of children having the same *achievement* level, the teacher must adjust to widely differing ages and interests. A twelve-year-old boy and a six-year-old boy usually do not work well together, even though they have the same reading achievement, because their

[17] Ketcham and Lafitte, *op. cit.*, pp. 338-340.

interests are so divergent. Thus, each plan of organization presents its own values and its own problems.

Using the results of evaluation: solutions

Teachers of beginning reading have worked out their own practical solutions to this dilemma of individual differences, based on their own experiences—sometimes successful, sometimes unsuccessful—in coping with the range of abilities existing in their classrooms. In schools where standardized measuring instruments have not been used, the teacher may not have known the full extent of the difference—at least not in objective measuring units. But in all cases, the teacher has known, from pupil behavior and pupil response, that what works with one pupil does not necessarily work with another and that adjustment to individual differences needs to be made. *And through the evaluation the teacher can group the children according to interest & mental age*

Systems of grouping. In graded school systems, horizontal grouping schemes have been used by almost all teachers in one form or another at some time. For certain types of activities, to be sure, the total group has seemed best. Among these activities for the total group are: news time, story hour, music, films, excursions, parties, special day celebrations, and even some types of pre-reading games. However, development of specific skills is a different kind of problem, a different teaching task requiring a different handling. Many teachers have adopted a three-group system, attempting to group children according to their general level of aptitude for the particular skill being taught. Such grouping is done usually on the basis of results of diagnostic tests of various kinds, as well as observations of day-to-day behavior. Some teachers use a mastery test as a basis for such grouping. A mastery test produces a profile of each pupil's level of mastery of each of the several skills that have been stressed in the immediately preceding period of instruction. This information thus serves as a working basis for grouping for succeeding skill-building activities.

Groups are usually kept as flexible as possible. Children are regrouped as their abilities in various skill areas shift in relation to abilities of the other pupils in the room and in relation to their own skills and abilities in other areas. Even specific types of practice from day to day frequently suggest temporary regroupings.

Such horizontal groupings provide for individual differences in instructional needs, but they do not solve the problem of moving pupils across grade lines. The kindergarten teacher and the first-grade teacher are still limited in their adjustive techniques to the "one year to one grade" framework of the vertical structure.

Some solutions for crossing grade lines have been tried, although these have been more often attempted at the middle-grade level than at the beginning levels. For example, teachers in Joplin, Missouri,[18] found the range of reading abilities in their middle grades to be from low second grade to ninth grade. Regrouping the same pupils across grade lines for purposes of reading instruction made it possible— with the same number of teachers—to create nine groups, each of which represented a reading-grade range of less than one year. In another middle-grade situation, three fourth-grade classes were considered a unit for cross-class grouping.[19] With reading scores ranging from 2.6 to 7.6 in the total fourth-grade group, it was possible, by using the same number of teachers and a system of cross-class grouping, to arrange the same pupils in six groups, most of which had a reading-age range of only one or two years. The widest range within a single group (3.2 years) occurred at the top level (from 4.4 to 7.6) and could probably have been avoided had the program of cross-class grouping been extended into the fifth and sixth grades.

Most such cross-class plans have been developed for the middle grades—perhaps because individual differences first become starkly apparent at that level. The fact is that the problems exist much earlier. As has been pointed out, chil-

[18] Cecil Floyd, "Meeting Children's Reading Needs in the Middle Grades: A Preliminary Report," *Elementary School Journal*, 55 (October 1954), 99-103.

[19] I. E. Aaron, Francis Goodwin, and Vada Kent, "Fourth Grade Teachers Experiment with Cross-Class Grouping for Reading Instruction," *Elementary English*, 36 (May 1959), 305-307.

dren entering school for the first time bring with them individual characteristics, producing in the typical beginner group a difference in mental age of at least four years.

Because of this wide difference in mental age, the point of readiness for learning a certain skill—the "teachable moment," as some educators call it—occurs at no specific chronological age and at no predetermined point in a school program. Nor do successive "teachable moments" in a ladder of skills occur at predictable intervals, since learning rate is a function of intellectual power.

Team teaching. Intra-class grouping helps a teacher at a given moment to reduce the range of individual differences within an instructional group. It does not relieve the teacher or the pupils of the pressure to conform to the curriculum prescribed for the grade or to the time limits set for mastery of certain skills. As a solution to these problems, a number of school systems are now trying an ungraded primary unit combined with team teaching. Team teaching may involve the cooperation of two or more regular teachers whose classrooms are connected or adjacent, or it may be a more complex organization with a team leader and senior teacher, in addition to a number of regular teachers.

Specifically, the advantages of team teaching for the problem of teaching beginning reading may be shown in simple mathematical form. Various phases of the pre-reading and beginning-reading program are the concern of the teachers of kindergarten, Grade 1, and Grade 2. Using an intra-class system of grouping, each of these teachers may attempt to teach three groups. That is, the three teachers will have a total of nine instructional groups at a given moment. There may be, and usually is, a large amount of overlapping among these nine groups as far as individual ability to learn is concerned. The top group in the kindergarten may well be able to do work of the same difficulty level as the lower group in Grade 1. Similarly the top group in Grade 1 may very likely be able to do work equivalent to that of the lower group in Grade 2. Because of prescribed standards and materials for these grades, these groups are probably not doing equivalent work, although their degree of "readiness" would indicate that they could and probably should be doing so.

With a team-teaching approach within a nongraded primary unit, it is frequently possible to reduce the total number of instructional groups while at the same time improving the instruction for the individual child. If careful and continuous evaluation of individual levels of readiness is made, then the pupils constituting the nine groups in a rigidly graded program may be regrouped into perhaps five or six groups better suited to individual needs than were the nine. Essential at all times is a flexible and sensitive program of regrouping in response to each individual's rate of progress in specific skill areas. If this kind of flexibility can be maintained, then there are no artificial barriers to progress nor any undue pressures on slow learners.

Thus the combination of good evaluation procedures, team teaching, and free movement upward (based on readiness for the next level of difficulty) provides an instructional setting in which the goal of continuous progress seems fairly close to realization. No child needs to jump a hurdle into another grade before he is prepared to do so; no child needs to waste his time waiting for others in his grade to catch up. Each pupil moves along at the rate to which his rate of learning suits him. Children of five may be found who will profit from formal instruction. Some children of six and seven may prove to be less able to respond to formal reading instruction than some of the younger pupils. Keeping the concept of the teachable moment in mind, the teacher may discuss with other members of her team the best placement of a certain pupil in order to insure his progress at his own maximum rate of learning. Successive team conferences, combined with the findings from the evaluation program, will provide for sensitive and flexible regroupings of children as individual differences in learning rate emerge.

Individual differences remain.   Regardless of the system of organization used by the school, the vast differences among individuals remain and, as was pointed out earlier, increase as instructional experiences continue. With any system of grouping—intra-class or cross-class or primary unit—brighter pupils will progressively outdistance slower pupils, widening rather than narrowing the gaps between them. The more effectively the organizational system permits continuous progress, the more visible become the differences among children, as realistic groupings place pupils with learning-mates, not necessarily with age-mates.

Children themselves are usually happier to be working at a level that is comfortable for them, but the children's happiness is not the only factor to be considered. Parents are frequently displeased if their child is not studying with his age-mates. Some parents are more concerned that their child keeps up with the Jones boy next door than that he is working at his own appropriate level. This conflict in school-child-parent goals seems to be built into our social structure, and those who plan educational programs must reckon with it. The school program cannot change the conflict, but it can minimize some school-parent misunderstanding through its procedures for reporting to parents.

The report-card system has traditionally been used as a means of letting parents know how well or how poorly their children are getting along. Other systems include conferences with parents, more extensive explanatory written reports, and combinations of these devices. In some school systems meetings with small groups of parents are scheduled. Such group meetings save the teacher time and also provide an atmosphere for discussion that some parents find more congenial than a private meeting. Group conferences cannot take the place of individual conferences, but they can reduce the number of individual conferences needed and can give parents—much earlier in the school year than might otherwise be possible—some understanding of the goals of classroom instruction and the day-to-day methods that are being used to achieve those goals.

ORGANIZATION SETS THE STAGE FOR INSTRUCTION

The materials in this chapter have dealt with the relation of organization and of administrative procedure to instruction. As has been pointed out, effective administration and organization can help to ensure the success of the pre-reading and the beginning-reading program. Flexible working groups can facilitate continuous progress. Cumulative records, including informal and formal test results of all kinds, can provide guidance at each level of planning. Also good relations between parents and school, with a mutual understanding of goals, can help to provide an atmosphere conducive to success in the classroom.

But all of these organizational and administrative devices only set the stage. The purpose for which all of the pre-planning exists is the daily instructional program, created by the genius of the teacher, based on her knowledge of her materials and her methods and on her understanding of her children.

This instruction, even for the beginning pupil, is not a thing to be adequately served up by the novice. Some learning will, of course, take place almost without planning; but the teacher who stands in the best position to do an effective instructional job is the teacher who *knows*—knows the range of activities she may use; knows her pupils and their limitations as well as their abilities; knows the basic attitudes, habits, and skills that are crucial in learning to read; knows what activities and what games are useful for building which skills; knows how growth takes place in relation to the methods she uses; and, most especially, knows how to choose and order the many possible classroom procedures that will enable her to provide for maximum growth for each individual child.

Informality at the early stages of instruction is always important. The fact that the teacher must plan carefully does not mean that the child needs to feel aware of the plan. Games and activities may all be casually and enjoyably introduced, letting natural motivation play its part as it does in other games and activities of childhood. No small child should ever feel compelled to achieve at a level beyond his own maturity. But the planning that lies behind the instruction, based on a knowledge of skill-activity relationships as described in this book, is vital to the development of a sharply focused pre-reading program.

BIBLIOGRAPHY

Aaron, I. E.; Goodwin, Frances; and Kent, Vada. "Fourth Grade Teachers Experiment with Cross-Class Grouping for Reading Instruction," *Elementary English*, 36 (May 1959), 305-307. Reports a fourth-grade experiment that appeared to demonstrate several advantages of a cross-class approach to grouping for reading instruction. The enthusiasm of the teachers was recognized as a factor in determining the outcome of the experiment.

D'Evelyn, Katherine E. *Individual Parent-Teacher Conferences; a Manual for Teachers of Young Children.* New York: Teachers College, Columbia University, 1945. A manual designed to help teachers analyze their parent conferences. Actual parent-teacher conferences covering a wide range of problems are analyzed, with attention being given to what should and should not be done.

Floyd, Cecil. "Meeting Children's Reading Needs in the Middle Grades: A Preliminary Report," *Elementary School Journal*, 55 (October 1954), 99-103. A report on the system of grouping used in Joplin, Missouri, in an effort to adjust to individual levels of reading achievement. Includes comments of both parents and pupils.

Goodlad, John I. "Individual Differences and Vertical Organization of the School," *Individualizing Instruction* (NSSE 61st Yearbook, Part I), 209-238. Chicago: National Society for the Study of Education and The University of Chicago Press, 1962. Analyzes the function of school organization in relation to individual differences and the goals of the public schools. Includes a summary of the steps that have been taken in the development of continuous progress plans.

————, and Anderson, Robert H. *The Nongraded Elementary School.* New York: Harcourt, Brace and World, Inc., 1959. Discusses the effects of nonpromotion in graded school systems; how the lock-step of graded structure developed; modern theories of curriculum development; home-school reporting; and the relationship between school standards and mental health. Describes the trend toward nongraded structures and offers suggestions for initiating and administering a nongraded school.

William S. Gray, ed. *Adjusting Reading Programs to Individuals (*University of Chicago Conference on Reading). Chicago: University of Chicago Press, 1941. Considers the characteristics of learners that affect the reading program and some of the administrative provisions that can be made for individual differences. Each part includes a section devoted specifically to the problems encountered in the primary grades.

Hardin, Garrett. *Nature and Man's Fate*. Holt, Rinehart & Winston, Inc., 1959. A genetic explanation of the nature and extent of individual differences. Valuable background reading for any teacher who has time to explore the biological bases of human behavior.

Ketcham, Warren A., and Lafitte, Rondeau G., Jr. "How Well Are They Learning?" *Educational Leadership*, 16 (March 1959), 337-341, 350. Presents longitudinal records of children's mental ages and reading ages, showing the range of individual differences at each chronological age.

Shane, Harold G. "The School and Individual Differences," *Individualizing Instruction* (NSSE 61st Yearbook, Part I), 55-61. Chicago: National Society for the Study of Education and The University of Chicago Press, 1962. Discusses trends in school organization as related to individual differences. Includes a list of thirty-five different approaches to grouping that have been developed in an effort to personalize teaching and to recognize individual differences.

Sheldon, William D. "Teaching the Very Young to Read," *The Reading Teacher*, 16 (December 1962), 163-169. Discusses the kinds of learning that are appropriate at various age levels.

Stock, Earl K. "Some Field Observations on Early-Grade Progress in Reading," *Elementary School Journal*, 55 (May 1955), 517-521. Discusses instruction in reading in relation to individual differences.

Index